Pittsburgh Series in Bibliography

MARGARET FULLER

Margaret Fuller

A DESCRIPTIVE BIBLIOGRAPHY.

Joel Myerson

UNIVERSITY OF
PITTSBURGH PRESS
1978

9/1979
Am. Lit.

Published by the University of Pittsburgh Press, Pittsburgh, Pa. 15260
Copyright © 1978, University of Pittsburgh Press
Feffer and Simons, Inc., London
Manufactured in the United States of America

Library of Congress Cataloging in Publication Data

Myerson, Joel.
  Margaret Fuller: a descriptive bibliography.

  (Pittsburgh series in bibliography)
  Includes index.
    1. Ossoli, Sarah Margaret Fuller, marchesa d',
  1810–1850—Bibliography. I. Series.
  Z8648.13.M92 |PS2506| 016.818'3'09   78-4203
  ISBN 0-8229-3381-0

To my parents
Edward and Gwenne Myerson

Contents

Acknowledgments

THIS bibliography is part of my ongoing study of American Transcendentalism. In compiling it I have incurred many debts of gratitude. Unhappily, I can only thank in a general way the many librarians who answered my questions about copies of Fuller's works at their institutions. I wish to express my appreciation to the following libraries and their staffs for help in using their collections: Boston Athenæum, Boston Public Library, Concord Free Public Library, Fruitlands Museums, Harvard University Libraries (Andover-Harvard Theological, Houghton, Schlesinger, and Widener libraries), Massachusetts Historical Society, The Newberry Library, and Northwestern University Library. The University of South Carolina Library has also been useful, and Beverly Brooks and Claudia Drum were both patient and skillful in obtaining books for me on loan.

Many people have helped me in this project and I would like especially to thank the following: William R. Cagle, John D. Cushing, Rodney G. Dennis, George Hall, William Henry Harrison, Carolyn Jakeman, Richard Colles Johnson, James Lawton, Carlton Lowenberg, Artem Lozynsky, Charles W. Mann, Marcia Moss, and Constance Fuller Threinen. I thank Louise Craft for her skillful editing of this book. I was first introduced to this period in American literary history by Harrison Hayford and my debt to him, for friendship and advice, will always be great.

The bibliographical groundwork for many nineteenth-century American authors was laid by Jacob Blanck in his *Bibliography of American Literature.* Like other scholars I have been greatly aided by his work.

Robert N. Hudspeth saved me much time through his unstinting help, and I am deeply in his debt for allowing me to view the materials he has assembled in preparing his forthcoming edition of Fuller's letters.

Matthew J. Bruccoli has been generous with his assistance and this bibliography is much better for it. His general advice and published work have been especially valuable in helping me to establish my format and terminology. Jennifer McCabe Atkinson and G. Thomas Tanselle read an earlier draft of this bibliography and my work has profited immensely from their informed suggestions.

I am fortunate to work at an institution that encourages and supports scholarship. For providing financial assistance and release time, I am grateful to the Research and Productive Scholarship Fund, the Department of English, and the College of Arts and Letters of the University of South Carolina. I am particularly indebted to Bert Dillon, William H. Nolte, Roger Sargent, the late John R. Welsh, and Calhoun Winton. I also wish to thank the following students and research assistants: R. Michael Barrett, Kaye Campbell, James

Ervin, Robert Hungerford, Robert Morace, Zenobia Rhue, Ronald Smoak, and especially, Robert Burkholder.

I am grateful to the following for permission to quote from manuscripts in their possession: Boston Public Library, Detroit Public Library, Houghton Library of Harvard University, and Little, Brown and Company. I am equally grateful to the following libraries for permission to reproduce photographs of materials in their possession: Henry E. Huntington Library, Houghton Library of Harvard University, Schlesinger Library of Radcliffe College, University of California at Los Angeles Library, University of Virginia Library, and Yale University Library.

Introduction

T H I S first comprehensive primary bibliography of Sarah Margaret Fuller, Marchesa d'Ossoli, provides an analytical description of all book-length publications by Fuller and lists all her known contributions to magazines, newspapers, and collections.[1]

FORMAT

Section A lists chronologically all books, pamphlets, and broadsides wholly or substantially by Fuller—including all printings of all editions in English.

The numbering system for Section A indicates the edition and printing for each entry. Thus for *Conversations with Goethe, A 2.1.a* indicates that this is the second title published by Fuller and that the entry describes the first edition *(1),* first printing *(a).* Issues are indicated by superior numbers—thus *A 6.1.a*[3] is the third issue of the first printing of the first edition of *Papers on Literature and Art.* States have been discovered in only one book, *Papers on Literature and Art,* and they are discussed in the text.

Section B lists chronologically all writings, including translations, by Fuller appearing in collections. Included are first appearances as well as reprinted items.

Section C lists chronologically all writings by Fuller appearing in magazines and newspapers during her lifetime. Included are reprinted materials. Fuller's contributions to the *Dial* are not signed with her name; authorship is assigned on the basis of evidence presented in my studies of the *Dial.*[2] Her contributions to the *New-York Tribune* are, unless otherwise noted, signed with an asterisk (*), her mark of authorship. Page and column locations are given for first appearances of Fuller's writings in the *New-York Tribune*—thus *p. 1:1–3* indicates that Fuller's contribution is on the first page in the first through third columns. A supplemental Section CC covers marginal items, which possibly are by Fuller but cannot be attributed to her with certainty.

An *appendix* lists principal works about Fuller.

---

1. For writings about Fuller, see Joel Myerson, *Margaret Fuller: An Annotated Secondary Bibliography* (New York: Burt Franklin & Co., 1977).

2. See especially Joel Myerson, "An Annotated List of Contributions to the Boston *Dial,"* *Studies in Bibliography,* 26 (1973), 133–166.

TERMS AND METHODS

Edition. All the copies of a book printed from a single setting of type—including all reprintings from standing type, from plates, or by photo-offset processes.

Printing. All the copies of a book printed at one time (without removing the type or plates from the press).

State. States occur only within single printings and are created by an alteration not affecting the conditions of issue to *some* copies of a given printing (by stop-press correction or cancellation of leaves). The only states for Fuller occur in *Papers on Literature and Art* (A 6).

Issue. All copies prepared for distribution (or marketing) in a fashion that clearly and purposefully differentiates them from other copies within the same printing. The classic definition of *issue,* applied to changes in the sheets of a book, derives from Renaissance printing techniques and fails to cover all the problems of nineteenth-century American book publishing; my definition is, therefore, formulated upon the evidence I have observed in Fuller's publications. Every instance of an issue, as defined here and as applied to Fuller's works, constitutes a definite and purposeful attempt by a publisher to *issue* (or put on sale) a number of copies in a distinct format. Within the context of most mid-nineteenth-century American publishing practices, and especially in Fuller's case, different issues (or distribution formats) clearly indicate important facts about the title's reception and sales; to relegate this information to a minor subcategory, such as *binding variants,* would be to obscure its value as evidence about an author's career.

English editions are indicated by the letter *E* after the edition number—thus A 5.1E.a is the first printing of the first English edition of *Woman in the Nineteenth Century.* The one German edition that turned up during extensive searching for foreign-language editions is indicated by the letter *G* after the edition number (see A 7.1G).

Dust jackets for Section A entries have been described in detail because they are part of the original publication effort and sometimes provide information about how the book was marketed. There is, of course, no certainty that a jacket now on a book was always on it.

For binding-cloth designations I have used the method proposed by Tanselle;[3] most of these cloth grains are illustrated in Jacob Blanck, ed., *Bibliography of American Literature* (New Haven: Yale University Press, 1955–).

Color specifications are based on the *ISCC-NBS Color Name Charts Illustrated with Centroid Colors* (National Bureau of Standards). Centroid numbers have not been assigned; instead, I have used the general color designations.[4]

---

3. G. Thomas Tanselle, "The Specifications of Binding Cloth," *The Library,* 21 (September 1966), 246–247.

4. See G. Thomas Tanselle, "A System of Color Identification for Bibliographical Description," *Studies in Bibliography,* 20 (1967), 203–234, for a discussion of how this system can be fully employed. I feel, however, that the use of exact Centroid designations creates a false sense of precision, especially for nineteenth-century books. Oxidation, fading, wear, and nonuniform dyeing practices make precise color identification difficult, if not impossible. In any case color identification by the Centroid system is inexact.

The spines of bindings or dust jackets are printed horizontally unless otherwise stipulated. The reader is to assume that vertically printed spines read from top to bottom, unless otherwise stipulated.

In the descriptions of title pages, bindings, and dust jackets, the color of the lettering is always black, unless otherwise stipulated.

The term *perfect binding* refers to books in which the pages are held together with adhesive along the back edge after the folds have been trimmed off—for example, most paperbacks.

The descriptions do not include leaf thickness or sheet bulk because there is no case for Fuller in which these measurements are required to differentiate printings.

This bibliography is based mainly upon evidence gathered from my personal inspection and collation of multiple copies of Fuller's works. Libraries holding copies that are bibliographically intact (not rebound or repaired) are listed. Exceptions are rebound copies containing nonbibliographical information, such as dated owners' inscriptions, which are mentioned in notes. The symbols used for American and Canadian libraries are those employed by the National Union Catalog; those for British libraries are the same as those listed in the *British Union-Catalogue of Periodicals,* which are here preceded by *B.* The following are additional symbols:

BLLL: The London Library, London
JM: Collection of Joel Myerson
MGb: Mason Library, Great Barrington, Mass.
MGro: Groton Public Library, Groton, Mass.
MHarF: Fruitlands Museums, Harvard, Mass.
MLen: Lenox Library Association, Lenox, Mass.
MMar: Marlborough Public Library, Marlborough, Mass.
MMel: Melrose Public Library, Melrose, Mass.
MNatM: Morse Institute, Natick, Mass.
MRea: Reading Public Library, Reading, Mass.
MWay: Wayland Free Public Library, Wayland, Mass.
MWin: Winthrop Public Library, Winthrop, Mass.
VtSjA: St. Johnsbury Athenæum, St. Johnsbury, Vt.

This bibliography is not an attempt to indicate the scarcity of Fuller's works and should not be taken as such. If there is one location listed, it means that of all the libraries I visited and corresponded with, only one had or reported having a copy with all the examined points intact; it does not mean that there is only one copy of that work in existence. For recent editions (A 13–A 16) I have not listed as many locations as for earlier ones, where I have tried to be as comprehensive as possible.

A bibliography is outdated the day it goes to the printer. Addenda and corrigenda are earnestly solicited.

The University of South Carolina
26 January 1977

A. Separate Publications

A 1 [PROSPECTUS FOR LANGUAGE CLASSES]
Only edition, only printing (1836)

Boston,   *October, 1836.*

IT is proposed by the Subscriber, to give instruction to classes of Ladies in GERMAN, ITALIAN, and FRENCH LITERATURE. Her wish is, to read, *with her Classes*, selections from the best authors, and to give them, at the same time, such general information, historical and critical, as may render their studies interesting, and facilitate their progress in acquiring a knowledge of the literature of those languages. Having often, herself, been impeded in such pursuits by obstacles, which might easily have been removed, by the aid of *oral instruction*, from one who had previously traversed the same ground, she hopes to give such assistance to those, who attend her, as will relieve them from similar embarrassments, and enable them, with ease and pleasure, to appropriate some part of the treasures of thought, which are contained in the classical works of foreign living languages. Fully to accomplish this object, it is desirable, that the pupil should become somewhat familiar with the style of the prominent writers of those nations, at different eras in their literary history. She does not propose to instruct in writing or speaking the languages; but, if there should be ladies who are desirous of learning to read them, preparatory to the above more advanced course of study, she is willing to form classes for that purpose.

After conversing with her friends upon the subject, she has adopted this method of addressing them, and those who may wish to receive such instruction. She wishes to make arrangements for giving lessons on the 1st of November next, and for that purpose, she has taken rooms at No. 2, Avon Place; where she invites those who wish to join either of her Classes, or to obtain more minute information upon the subject, to call upon her on that day, or afterwards. In the mean time, any written application addressed to her, at that place, will receive attention.

Respectfully,

SARAH MARGARET FULLER.

REGULATIONS.

1. Separate Classes will be formed, for each language, in which instruction is given.
2. Two lessons will be given to each Class, every week, at such hours and on such days, as shall be found most convenient, upon consultation with its members.
3. The price will be fifteen dollars for a course of twenty-four lessons.

A 1: $9^{15}/_{16}'' \times 8^1/_{16}''$

$9^{15}/_{16}'' \times 8^1/_{16}''$; pink wove paper; recto: text; verso, blank.

Location: MH.

A 2 CONVERSATIONS WITH GOETHE

A 2.1.a
Only edition, first printing (1839)

CONVERSATIONS WITH GOETHE

IN THE LAST YEARS OF HIS LIFE,

TRANSLATED FROM THE GERMAN

OF

ECKERMANN.

By S. M. FULLER.

BOSTON:
HILLIARD, GRAY, AND COMPANY.

M.DCCC.XXXIX.

A 2.1.a: 7⁵/₁₆″ × 4¹¹/₁₆″

Two issues have been noted.

A 2.1.a¹
First issue

[i–vii] viii–xxvi [xxvii–xxviii] [1–3] 4–27 [28–31] 32–414 [415–416]

[a]⁶ b⁸ A–I⁶ K–Z⁶ AA–II⁶ KK⁴

Contents: p. i: 'SPECIMENS | OF | FOREIGN STANDARD LITERATURE. | VOL. IV.'; p. ii: blank; p. iii: 'SPECIMENS | OF | FOREIGN STANDARD LITERATURE. | EDITED | BY GEORGE RIPLEY. | [rule] | VOL. IV. | CONTAINING | CONVERSATIONS WITH GOETHE, | FROM THE GERMAN | OF | ECKERMANN. | [rule] | BOSTON: | HILLIARD, GRAY, AND COMPANY. | [rule] | M.DCCC.XXXIX.'; p. iv: 'As wine and oil are imported to us from abroad, so must ripe | understanding, and many civil virtues, be imported into our | minds from foreign writings;—we shall else miscarry/still, and | come short in the attempts of any great enterprise. | MILTON, *History of Britain, Book III.*'; p. v: title page; p. vi: 'Entered according to Act of Congress, in the/year 1839, | BY HILLIARD, GRAY, AND CO. | in the Clerk's Office of the District Court of the District of Massachusetts. | STEREOTYPED AT THE | BOSTON TYPE AND STEREOTYPE FOUNDRY.'; pp. vii–xxvi: 'TRANSLATOR'S PREFACE.' signed 'JAMAICA PLAINS, *May* 23, 1839.'; p. xxvii: contents; p. xxviii: blank; p. 1: 'ECKERMANN.'; p. 2: blank; pp. 3–414: text; pp. 415–416: blank.

Typography and paper: 7⁵/₁₆″ × 4¹¹/₁₆″; wove paper; 32 lines per page. Running heads: rectos: pp. ix–xxv: 'TRANSLATOR'S PREFACE.'; pp. 5–7: 'AUTHOR'S PREFACE.'; pp. 9–27: 'INTRODUCTION.'; pp. 33–413: 'CONVERSATIONS.'; versos: pp. viii–xxvi: 'TRANSLATOR'S PREFACE.'; pp. 4–414: 'ECKERMANN.'.

Binding: Cloth and color variations listed below. Front and back covers: blank. Spine: printed paper label: 'SPECIMENS | OF | FOREIGN | LITERATURE. | IV. | [rule] | ECKERMANN. | CONVERSATIONS | WITH GOETHE. | [rule] | TRANSLATED BY | S. M. FULLER. | [rule] | COMPLETE IN ONE VOLUME.' in black. Flyleaves. Off white endpapers. All edges trimmed.

1. Dark gray blue P cloth (pebble-grained).
   Locations: JM, MeB, NGenoU, TxU.
2. Dark green P cloth (pebble-grained).
   Locations: MH, MMeT, MWA, OKentU, PPA, RHi, ViU, VtU.
3. Gray olive green HC cloth (hexagon-grained).
   Locations: JM, MH.

Publication: Listed in *North American Review,* 49 (July 1839), 271. Reviewed in *New York Review,* 5 (July 1839), 233–234. Inscribed copies: OKentU (May 1839), MWA (20 May 1839). The dating of the inscription in the MWA copy—three days prior to the date of the "Translator's Preface"—is undoubtedly in error.

Note one: A copy bound in green P cloth (pebble-grained), lacking the title and half-title pages carrying the *Specimens* identification, apparently a binding error of no significance, has been noted: LNHT.

Note two: A copy bound in dark brown S cloth (fine-ribbed), with goldstamped 'ECKERMANN'S | CONVERSATIONS | WITH | GOETHE' on the spine, has been noted: PSt. Possibly a remainder binding.

A 2.1.a²
Second issue

Pp. i–iv (leafs a$_{1,2}$), identifying the volume as part of the *Specimens* series, have been canceled. Pp. v–416 are the same as in the first issue.

Typography and paper: 7⁵/₁₆″ × 4¹¹/₁₆″; all else same as in the first issue.

Binding: Dark gray green C cloth (coarse sand-grained). Front and back covers: blank. Spine: printed paper label, same as in the first issue, except 'SPECIMENS | OF | FOREIGN | LITERATURE | IV.' was excised before the label was affixed to the spine. All edges trimmed.

Location: JM.

Note: Possibly a remainder binding.

A 2.1.b
Second printing (1852)

CONVERSATIONS WITH GOETHE | IN THE LAST YEARS OF HIS LIFE, | TRANS-LATED FROM THE GERMAN | OF | ECKERMANN. | BY S. M. FULLER, | (MARCHESA OSSOLI.) | NEW EDITION. | BOSTON AND CAMBRIDGE: | JAMES MUNROE AND COMPANY. | 1852.

[1–27⁸ 28⁴]

Contents: p. iii: 'ECKERMANN'S CONVERSATIONS.'; p. iv: blank; p. v: title page; pp. 6–414: same as in the first printing.

Typography and paper: 7″ × 4¹/₂″; all else same as in the first printing.

Binding: Brown S cloth (fine-ribbed). Front and back covers: blindstamped triple-ruled border with leaf in each corner and 3¹/₂″ ornament in center. Spine: blind-stamped filigree design with goldstamped 'ECKERMANN'S | CONVERSATIONS | WITH | GOETHE | [rule] | S. M. FULLER.'; variations listed below. Flyleaves. Yellow endpapers. All edged trimmed.

1. 'S. M. FULLER' is in gothic type.
   Location: VtNN.
2. 'S. M. FULLER' is in roman type.
   Location: CaOLU.

Publication: Listed in *Christian Examiner*, 52 (May 1852), 458.

GÜNDERODE.

~~~~~~~~~~~

Our communion was sweet,—it was the epoch in which I first became conscious of myself.

The kingdom in which we met sank down like a cloud, parting to receive us to a secret Paradise:—there all was new—surprising, but congenial to spirit and heart; and thus the days went by.

~~~~~~~~~~~

BOSTON:
PUBLISHED BY E. P. PEABODY,
No. 109 Washington Street.
1842.

A 3: 7³/₁₆″ × 4³/₈″

[i–v] vi–vii [viii] ix–xii [1] 2–106 [107–108]

[a]² 1*⁶ 1*⁴ 2–9⁶

Contents: p. i: 'GÜNDERODE.'; p. ii: blank; p. iii: title page; p. iv: 'Entered according to Act of Congress, in the year 1842, by | E. P. PEABODY, | in the Clerk's Office of the District Court of Massachusetts. | WM. WHITE & H. P. LEWIS, | PRINTERS, | OVER BOSTON TYPE FOUNDRY, SPRING LANE.'; pp. v–vii: 'TRANSLATOR'S PREFACE.' dated 'BOSTON, 10th March 1842'; pp. viii–xii: 'PREFACE.' ['As many readers may be unacquainted with the name of Günderode, the following extract is given from an article in the Dial . . . entitled "Bettine Brentano and her friend Günderode." ']; pp. 1–106: text; pp. 107–108: blank.

Typography and paper: 7³/₁₆″ × 4³/₈″; wove paper; 33 lines per page. Running heads: rectos: pp. vii–xi: 'PREFACE.'; pp. 3–105: 'GÜNDERODE.'; versos: pp. vi–xii: 'PREFACE.'; pp. 2–106: 'GÜNDERODE.'.

Binding: Tan paper wrappers with black printing. Front wrapper, recto: 'GÜNDERODE: | A TRANSLATION FROM THE GERMAN. | [rule] | BOSTON: | PUB-LISHED BY E. P. PEABODY | No. 109 Washington Street, | 1842.', within a double-ruled border. Front wrapper, verso: 'NOTICE' of subscription terms to future numbers of this translation. Back wrapper, recto: list of books that Peabody 'PUBLISHES AND HAS FOR SALE'. Back wrapper, verso: blank. All edges trimmed.

Location: CSmH (lacks back wrapper), PSt (lacks front wrapper).

Publication: Fuller wrote Emerson on 8 March 1842: "I finished the 1ˢᵗ no Günderode last night, it will be out early next week" (*The Letters of Ralph Waldo Emerson,* ed. Ralph L. Rusk [New York: Columbia University Press, 1939], III, 29). Reviewed in *Arcturus,* 3 (May 1842), 470–472. Price: 37¹/₂¢. Inscribed copy: NNC [rebound] (24 March 1842).

Note one: A numbering error resulted in two signatures signed '1*'.

Note two: Copies rebound with wrappers have been noted: DLC, IEN, MB.

Note three: No more numbers were published, though four were planned. The trans-lation was completed by Mina Wesselhoeft and published as *Correspondence of Fräulein Günderode and Bettine von Arnim* by T. O. H. P. Burnham of Boston in 1861, with few changes made in Fuller's original translation.

GÜNDERODE:

A TRANSLATION FROM THE GERMAN.

BOSTON:
PUBLISHED BY E. P. PEABODY
No. 109 Washington Street,
1842.

Printed paper wrapper for A 3

A 4.1.a
First edition, first printing (1844)

SUMMER ON THE LAKES,

IN 1843.

BY

S. M. FULLER.

BOSTON:

CHARLES C. LITTLE AND JAMES BROWN.

NEW YORK:

CHARLES S. FRANCIS AND COMPANY.

MDCCCXLIV.

A 4.1.a: 7^{13}/$_{16}$″ × 4^{13}/$_{16}$″

Three issues have been noted.

A 4.1.a¹
First issue

[i–iv] [1–3] 4–13 [14] 15–42 [43] 44–69 [70] 71–108 [109] 110–168 [169] 170–236 [237] 238–256

[a]² 1–21⁶ 22²

Contents: p. i: 'SUMMER ON THE LAKES.'; p. ii: blank; p. iii: title page; p. iv: 'Entered according to the Act of Congress, in the year 1844, | By S. M. FULLER, | in the Clerk's Office of the District Court of the District of Massachusetts | BOSTON: | PRINTED BY FREEMAN AND BOLLES, | WASHINGTON STREET.'; p. 1: 'SUMMER ON THE LAKES. | [rule] | [Poem, 'SUMMER days of busy leisure . . .']'; p. 2: poem, 'To A Friend'; pp. 3–256: text.

Typography and paper: 7¹³/₁₆″ × 4¹³/₁₆″; wove paper; 32 lines per page. Running heads: rectos: pp. 5–13: 'NIAGARA.'; pp. 15–29: 'THE LAKES.'; pp. 31–35: 'CHICAGO.'; p. 37: 'GENEVA.'; p. 39: 'A THUNDER STORM.'; p. 41: 'PAPAW GROVE.'; pp. 45–47: 'ROCK RIVER.'; pp. 49–51: 'OREGON.'; p. 53: 'ANCIENT INDIAN VILLAGE.'; pp. 55–57: 'GANYMEDE.'; p. 59: 'OREGON.'; p. 61: 'WOMEN IN THE WEST.'; p. 63: 'EDUCATION.'; p. 65: 'KISHWAUKIE.'; p. 67: 'RETROSPECTION.'; p. 69: 'FAREWELL.'; p. 71: 'TRIFORMIS.'; pp. 73–75: 'THE PRAIRIES.'; p. 77: 'EVENING THOUGHTS.'; p. 79: 'HASTE MAKES WASTE.'; pp. 81–101: 'MARIANA.'; p. 103: 'PHILIP VAN ARTEVELDE.'; pp. 105–107: 'MORRIS BIRKBECK.'; p. 111: 'TITIAN'S VENUS AND ADONIS.'; p. 113: 'MILWAUKIE.'; p. 115: 'INDIAN ANECDOTE.'; p. 117: 'WOODS.'; p. 119: 'INDIAN ENCAMPMENT.'; p. 121: 'MILWAUKIE.'; p. 123: 'THE COTTAGE.'; p. 125: 'THE SEERESS OF PREVORST.'; p. 127: 'FREE HOPE.'; p. 129: 'OLD CHURCH.'; p. 131: 'SELF-POISE.'; pp. 133–163: 'THE SEERESS OF PREVORST.'; pp. 165–167: 'MILWAUKIE.'; pp. 171–183: 'MACKINAW.'; pp. 185–189: 'RECEPTION OF INDIAN CHIEFS.'; p. 191: 'EVERETT'S SPEECH.'; p. 193: 'MISSIONARIES.'; p. 195: 'OBSTACLES.'; p. 197: 'KEY-WAY-NO-WUT.'; p. 199: 'INDIAN ORATOR.'; p. 201: 'MRS. SCHOOLCRAFT.'; pp. 203–205: 'MUCKWA.'; p. 207: 'THE YOUNG WARRIOR.'; pp. 209–211: 'OLD ADAIR.'; p. 213: 'DEATH OF RED SHOES.'; p. 215: 'INDIAN CUSTOMS.'; pp. 217–219: 'CARVER.'; pp. 221–225: 'HENRY.'; p. 227: 'CARVER.'; p. 229: 'RED JACKET.'; p. 231: 'PETALESHARRO.'; p. 233: 'MACKENZIE.'; p. 235: 'M'KENNEY.'; p. 239: 'THE GENERAL SCOTT.'; p. 241: 'ST. JOSEPH'S.'; p. 243: 'EDITH.'; p. 245: 'RAPIDS.'; p. 247: 'DINNERS.'; p. 249: 'MACKINAW.'; p. 251: 'INDIANS.'; p. 253: 'GENERAL HULL.'; p. 255: 'THE BOOK TO THE READER.'; versos: pp. 4–256: 'SUMMER ON THE LAKES.'.

Binding: S cloth (fine-ribbed); color and stamping variations listed below. Spine: blindstamped bands and ornaments with goldstamped 'SUMMER | ON THE | LAKES'. Pink endpapers. All edges trimmed.

1. Black cloth; front and back covers: blindstamped filigree design of scroll across top and bottom.
   Locations: CaBViP, InNd, MC, MWA, MnDu, MnHi, NN, NNS, NRU, NSchU, OU, OrU, PMA, RPR, RWe, ViW, VtMiM.
2. Black cloth; front and back covers: blindstamped strapwork design with leafy sprays.
   Location: NbU.
3. Brown cloth; front and back covers: blindstamped filigree design of scroll across top and bottom.
   Locations: GEU, KyU, MWin, MeU, Mi, MoHi, NBu, NcGU, NcU, NjNbS, OkU, PSt.

4. Brown cloth; front and back covers: blindstamped strapwork design with leafy sprays.
Locations: MoHi, PU.

Publication: Little and Brown wrote Emerson on 29 May 1844 agreeing to publish *Summer on the Lakes,* paying Fuller 10 percent of the retail price of each copy sold, "the whole copyright . . . to be paid when enough of the book shall have been sold to pay us the costs of publication" (MH). Advertised as "This day published" in *Boston Daily Advertiser,* 4 June 1844, p. 3. Price: 75¢. Inscribed copies: MC (4 June 1844), ViW (6 June 1844), VtMiM (10 June 1844), PU (18 June 1844), NRU (22 June 1844). The copy at ViW is the former deposit copy at DLC and the date is the deposit date.

Note one: Listed under "New Works" received between 13 and 29 July in *Publishers' Circular and Booksellers' Record,* 7 (1 August 1844), 234, and priced at 7s. This probably refers to an importation of the American edition rather than a separate issue of the American sheets in English casings.

Note two: The text of *Summer on the Lakes,* much edited by Arthur B. Fuller and annotated by him with extracts from Fuller's manuscript journal of the trip, is included in *At Home and Abroad* (1856) (see A 9.1.a).

A 4.1.a²
Second issue

Plates have been inserted between pp. [ii]–[iii], 58–59, 72–73, 104–105, 118–119, 170–171, 248–249.

Binding: Same as in first issue.

Locations: Binding 1: BL, JM, MB, MLen, NSyU; binding 2: CU, CaOLU, CtY, DLC, InTl, JM, MWiW, WaS; binding 3: CtU, InU, MWA, NBuHi, NN, NhD, ViU; binding 4: ArU, CU-B, CtHT-W, ICHi, IMacoW, JM, KHi, OCl, PMA, ViU.

Publication: Fuller wrote Sarah Shaw that this issue was placed on sale somewhat later than the unillustrated one because the plates did not arrive until a number of copies had been bound (n.d., MH). Copies with the etchings were more expensive than those of the first issue (Fuller to Georgiana Bruce, 15 August 1844, MH). Inscribed copy: MH [rebound] (June 1844). Nearly 700 copies had been sold by the following year (Fuller to Richard Fuller, 9 January 1845, MH).

Note one: The copy at NN has the fifth plate inserted between pp. 108 and 109 and the copy at PMA lacks the third and fourth plates, apparently binding errors of no significance.

Note two: According to Sarah Clarke, a close friend of Fuller, "The etchings . . . were made by me at my own expense—I think the publisher took charge of the printing of them for the book" (letter of 23 November 1883 to T. W. Higginson, MB).

A 4.1.a³
Third issue

Sheets of the first issue (no plates) with Little and Brown title page in blue paper wrappers with black printing. Front wrapper, recto: 'SUMMER ON THE LAKES, | IN 1843. | BY | S. M. Fuller. | AUTHORESS OF WOMAN IN THE 19TH CENTURY. | [rule] | NEW-YORK: | W. H. GRAHAM, | Tribune Buildings. | [double dotted rules] | 1845.' within an ornamental border. Front wrapper, verso, and back wrapper, recto and verso: blank.

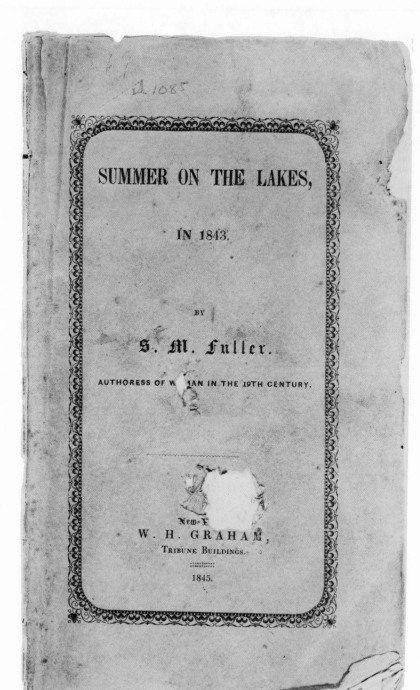

SUMMER ON THE LAKES,

IN 1843.

BY

S. M. Fuller.

AUTHORESS OF WOMAN IN THE 19TH CENTURY.

New-York.
W. H. GRAHAM,
TRIBUNE BUILDINGS.

1845.

Printed paper wrapper for A 4.1.a³

Location: MH.

Note: According to *New-York Daily Tribune,* 13 May 1845, p. 2, four hundred copies, probably remaindered, were to be placed on sale in New York by Graham. Fuller was by this time working for the *Tribune.*

SUBSEQUENT PRINTINGS

A 4.1.b
Second printing: New York: Haskell House, 1970.

Facsimile of the second issue.

A 4.1.c
Third printing: Nieuwkoop, the Netherlands: B. De Graaf, 1972.

Facsimile of the second issue. 500 copies printed.

A 4.1E
First English edition, only printing (1861)

SUMMER ON THE LAKES.

WITH AUTOBIOGRAPHY.

BY

MARGARET FULLER OSSOLI.

And Memoir,

BY

RALPH WALDO EMERSON, W. H. CHANNING,

AND OTHERS.

LONDON:

WARD AND LOCK, FLEET STREET.

MDCCCLXI.

A 4.1E: 6³/₈″ × 4″

[A]⁴ B–I⁸ K–Z⁸ [AA]⁴

Contents: p. i: title page; p. ii: blank; pp. iii–vi: 'PREFACE'; p. vii: contents; p. viii: blank; p. 1: poem, 'Summer days of busy leisure . . .'; p. 2: poem, 'To a Friend'; pp. 3–246: text of *Summer on the Lakes;* p. 247: 'MEMOIR | OF | MARGARET FULLER OSSOLI.'; p. 248: blank; pp. 249–360: text of *Memoirs* through 1840.

Typography and paper: 6³/₈″ × 4″; wove paper; 31 lines per page.

Binding: Illustrated boards. Front cover: printed in black, green, and red on yellow background, identification as part of British Library series, the title, price, publisher, and designs of United Kingdom national flowers and Royal Arms. Back cover: printed in black on yellow background, ad for British Library series. Spine: illustrated yellow strip with black printing: 'SUMMER | ON THE | LAKES | [rule] | THE | BRITISH | LIBRARY | TWO SHILLINGS'. All edges trimmed.

Locations: BO, CLU.

Publication: Advertised for "Early in September" in *Athenæum,* no. 1766 (31 August 1861), 268, and as among "New Books," no. 1767 (7 September 1861), 313. Announced as published between 31 August and 14 September in *Publishers' Circular and Booksellers' Record,* 24 (16 September 1861), 409. Price: 2s. Inscribed copy: BL [rebound] (deposit copy, 8 November 1861).

Note: The Ward and Lock advertisement in *Athenæum,* no. 1766 (31 August 1861), 268, promised a cloth issue priced at 2s. 6d.; no copies have been reported.

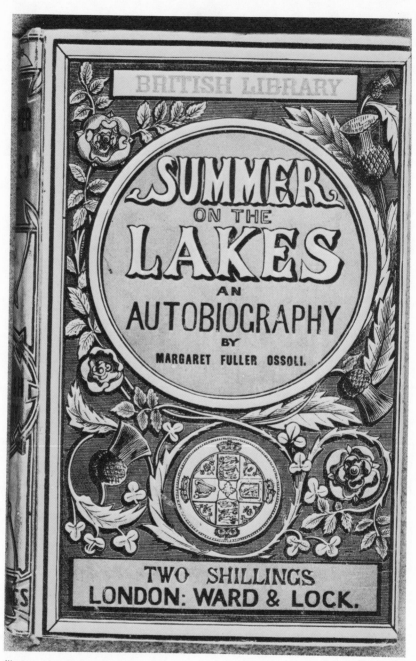

SUMMER ON THE LAKES

AN AUTOBIOGRAPHY

BY

MARGARET FULLER OSSOLI.

TWO SHILLINGS
LONDON: WARD & LOCK.

Illustrated boards for A 4.1E

A 5 WOMAN IN THE NINETEENTH CENTURY

A 5.1.a
First edition, only printing (1845)

WOMAN

IN THE

NINETEENTH CENTURY.

BY S. MARGARET FULLER.

" Frei durch Vernunft, stark durch Gesetze,
Durch Sanftmuth gross, und reich durch Schätze,
Die lange Zeit dein Busen dir verschwieg."

—

"I meant the day-star should not brighter rise,
Nor lend like influence from its lucent seat;
  I meant she should be courteous, facile, sweet,
Free from that solemn vice of greatness, pride ;
  I meant each softest virtue there should meet,
Fit in that softer bosom to reside ;
  Only a (heavenward and instructed) soul
I purposed her, that should, with even powers,
  The rock, the spindle, and the shears control
Of destiny, and spin her own free hours."

NEW-YORK:
GREELEY & McELRATH, 160 NASSAU-STREET.
W. Osborn, Printer, 88 William-street.
....
1845.

A 5.1.a: 7³/₄″ × 4¹/₂″

Two issues have been noted.

A 5.1.a¹
First issue

[i–v] vi [5] 6–164 [165–167] 168–201 [202]

[a]¹ [b]² 1–8¹² 9² [10]¹

Contents: p. i: snake and triangle device; p. ii: blank; p. iii: title page; p. iv: '[rule] |
Entered according to Act of Congress, in the year 1845, | BY S. MARGARET FULLER,
| In the Clerk's Office of the District Court of the Southern District of New-York. |
[rule]'; pp. v–vi: 'PREFACE.' dated *'November, 1844.'*; pp. 5–164: text dated '15*th*
November, 1844.'; p. 165: 'APPENDIX.'; p. 166: blank; pp. 167–201: appendix; p. 202:
blank.

Typography and paper: 7³/₄″ × 4¹/₂″; wove paper; 33 lines per page. Running heads:
rectos: pp. 7–25: 'NINETEENTH CENTURY.'; pp. 27–31: 'MIRANDA.'; p. 33: 'EMILY
PLATER.'; p. 35: 'EVE AND MARY.'; p. 37: 'LET ALL THE PLANTS GROW!'; p. 39:
'ISIS.'; p. 41: 'PORTIA.'; p. 43: 'WOMAN IN GREECE.'; p. 45: 'IN SPAIN.'; p. 47: 'RHINE
LEGEND.'; p. 49: 'WOMAN HAD ALWAYS HER SHARE OF POWER.'; p. 51: 'GIVE THE
LIBERTY OF LAW.'; p. 53: 'ELIZABETH, ISABELLA, AND MARINA.'; p. 55: 'ENGLISH
IDEALS.'; p. 57: 'LORD HERBERT.'; p. 59: 'WOMAN CAPABLE OF FRIENDSHIP.'; p.
61: 'MADAME ROLAND.'; p. 63: 'GEORGE SAND.'; p. 65: 'CAUSE OF ELOISA'S MIS-
TAKE.'; p. 67: 'WILLIAM AND MARY HOWITT.'; p. 69: 'HIGHEST GRADE OF UNION.';
p. 71: 'THE FLYING PIGEON.'; p. 73: 'XENOPHON'S PANTHEA.'; pp. 75–79: 'PAN-
THEA.'; p. 81: 'THE WIFE INEVITABLY INFLUENCES THE HUSBAND.'; p. 83:
'SCHOOL-INSTRUCTION.'; p. 85: 'OLD BACHELORS AND OLD MAIDS.'; p. 87: 'WHY
GROW OLD?'; p. 89: 'THE BETROTHED OF THE SUN.'; p. 91: 'TUNE THE LYRE.'; p.
93: 'CASSANRRA.'; p. 95: 'SEERESS OF PREVORST.'; p. 97: 'THE BRIBE IS NOT THE
PRIZE.'; p. 99: 'DR. CHANNING.'; p. 101: 'KINMONT AND SHELLEY.'; p. 103: 'EXCEP-
TIONS TO EVERY RULE.'; p. 105: 'PROCLUS TEACHES WELL.'; p. 107: 'CAN WE
TRUST AN EARTHLY FATHER?'; p. 109: 'SWEDENBORG'S VIEW.'; p. 111: 'FOURIER'S
VIEW.'; p. 113: 'THE DAUGHTERS OF GOETHE.'; p. 115: 'THE TRUE FELICITY.'; p.
117: 'MISS EDGEWORTH.'; p. 119: 'MEN WOULD NOT LISTEN TO MY VOICE.'; p. 121:
'THE LADY IN COMUS.'; p. 123: 'MAN IS NOT OF SATYR-DESCENT.'; p. 125:
'T[E]MPLE OF JUNO.'; p. 127: 'FOLLOW UNA, NOT DUESSA.'; p. 129: 'THE OLD MAN
ELOQUENT.'; p. 131: 'IMMORTAL EVE.'; p. 133: 'LIFT UP THE FALLEN.'; p. 135:
'EUGENE SUE.'; p. 137: 'A GRANDISON MUCH WANTED.'; p. 139: 'IS PURITY AN
EXOTIC?'; p. 141: 'EXALTADOS! EXALTADAS!'; p. 143: 'LOVE PARTS NOT WITH
IDUNA.'; p. 145: 'PARAGUAY WOMAN.'; p. 147: 'BOND-MAIDS! BRUNHILDAS!'; p.
149: 'MISS SEDGWICK.'; p. 151: 'THE O'CONNELL MASS.'; p. 153: 'ANNEXATION OF
TEXAS.'; p. 155: 'THE HEMISPHERES.'; p. 157: 'THE NEW DODONA!'; p. 159: 'IT WAS
THE MAN'S NOTION.'; p. 161: 'PERICLES AND ASPASIA.'; p. 163: 'BE TRUE TO-DAY.';
pp. 169–201: 'APPENDIX.'; versos: p. vi: 'PREFACE.'; pp. 6–24: 'WOMAN IN THE'; pp.
26–164: 'WOMAN IN THE NINETEENTH CENTURY.'; pp. 168–200: 'APPENDIX.'.

Binding: Light blue green paper wrappers with black printing. Front wrapper, recto:
same as title page, except

TITLE PAGE   WRAPPER

l. 27 [not present] | Price 50 Cents.

within double-ruled border with designs in each corner. Front wrapper, verso: ad for
Greeley & McElrath's Cheerful Books for the People series. Back wrapper, recto and
verso: blank. All edges trimmed.

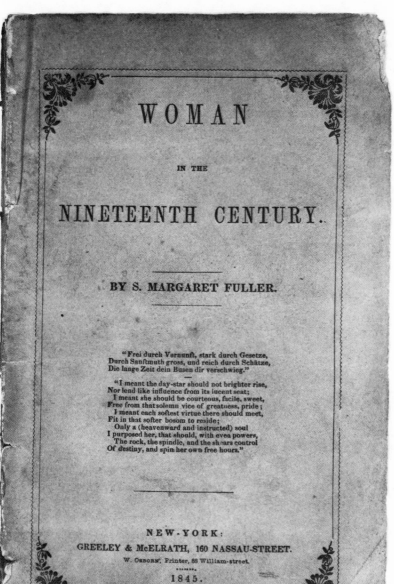

WOMAN

IN THE

NINETEENTH CENTURY.

BY S. MARGARET FULLER.

"Frei durch Vernunft, stark durch Gesetze,
Durch Sanftmuth gross, und reich durch Schätze,
Die lange Zeit dein Busen dir verschwieg."

"I meant the day-star should not brighter rise,
Nor lend like influence from its lucent seat;
I meant she should be courteous, facile, sweet,
Free from that solemn vice of greatness, pride;
I meant each softest virtue there should meet,
Fit in that softer bosom to reside;
Only a (heavenward and instructed) soul
I purposed her, that should, with even powers,
The rock, the spindle, and the shears control
Of destiny, and spin her own free hours."

NEW-YORK:
GREELEY & McELRATH, 160 NASSAU-STREET.
W. Osborn, Printer, 88 William-street.
1845.
Price 50 Cents.

Printed paper wrapper for A 5.1.a¹

Locations: DLC, MH, MHarF, MHi, MWA, ViU.

Publication: Horace Greeley wrote to Richard Fuller on 30 July 1855 that he thought 1,500 copies had been printed (MH). Mentioned as "in press" in *Boston Courier,* 8 February 1845, p. 2. Reviewed in *New-York Daily Tribune,* 13 February 1845, p. 1. Listed as a February publication in *Wiley & Putnam's Literary News-Letter,* March 1845, p. 303. Price: 50¢.

Note one: Greeley's 30 July 1855 letter states he "sold them out very soon" (MH); and according to A. P. Peabody, "the first edition . . . was soon exhausted, but the author's absence from the country prevented another edition at that time" (*North American Review,* 81 [October 1855], 558).

Note two: The text of *Woman in the Nineteenth Century,* much edited by Arthur B. Fuller with Greeley's aid, is included in *Woman in the Nineteenth Century, and Kindred Papers* (1855) (see A 8.1.a).

A 5.1.a²
Second issue

Typography and paper: 7⁵/₁₆″ × 4⁷/₁₆″; all else same as in the first issue.

Binding: Dark purple gray TB cloth (net-grained). Front and back covers: blank. Spine: printed paper label, 'WOMAN | IN THE | [two lines in German black letter] NINETEENTH | CENTURY. | BY | S. M. FULLER.' in black. Flyleaves. White endpapers. All edges trimmed.

Locations: MH-AH, MeBa.

Publication: Apparently published at the same time as the first issue. Price: 50¢.

Note: Possibly a remainder binding. Greeley wrote to Richard Fuller on 30 July 1855 that "we sold off most of the [original edition] and sold out the balance to a general publishing house" at a good price, "so as to close up the account and pay over what was coming" to Fuller (MH). Fuller wrote her brother Eugene on 9 March 1845 that the whole edition had been sold off to a bookseller and she had received eighty-five dollars as her share (MH).

A 5.1E.a
First English edition, first printing (1845)

WOMAN

IN THE

NINETEENTH CENTURY

BY S. MARGARET FULLER.

" Frei durch Vernunft, stark durch **Gesetze,**
Durch Sanftmuth gross, und reich durch **Schatze,**
Die lange Zeit dein Busen dir verschwieg."

"I meant the day-star should not **brighter rise,**
Nor lend like influence from its lucent seat;
I meant she should be courteous, facile, **sweet,**
Free from that solemn vice of greatness, **pride;**
I meant each softest virtue there should **meet,**
Fit in that softer bosom to reside;
Only a (heavenward and instructed) **soul**
I purposed her, that should, with even **powers,**
The rock, the spindle, and the shears **control**
Of destiny, and spin her own free hours."

LONDON:
H. G. CLARKE AND CO., 66, OLD BAILEY.

M.D.CCC.XLV.

A 5.1E.a: 6⁹/₁₆″ × 4⁵/₁₆″

[iii–v] vi–vii [viii] [9] 10–170 [171–173] 174–212 [1] 2–6 [7] 8 [9] 10 [11–12]

[A]⁸ B–I⁸ K–O⁸

Contents: p. iii: title page; p. iv: 'LONDON: | Reding and Judd, Printers, 4, Horse Shoe Court, Ludgate Hill.'; pp. v–vii: 'PREFACE.'; p. viii: blank; pp. 9–170: text; p. 171: 'APPENDIX.'; p. 172: blank; pp. 173–212: appendix; pp. 1–12: advertisements.

Typography and paper: 6⁹/₁₆″ × 4⁵/₁₆″; wove paper; 30 lines per page. Running heads: rectos: p. vi: 'PREFACE.'; pp. 11–169: 'NINETEENTH CENTURY.'; pp. 175–211: 'APPENDIX.'; versos: p. vii: 'PREFACE.'; pp. 10–170: 'WOMAN IN THE'; pp. 174–212: 'APPENDIX.'.

Binding: Red L cloth (diagonal-grained morocco). Front and back covers: blind-stamped triple-ruled border with ornaments in each corner and 2³/₄″ ornament in center. Spine: goldstamped '[rule] | [rule] | WOMAN | IN THE | 19TH | CENTURY | [rule] | [rule] | [ornate leaf and vine design]'. Pale green endpapers. All edges trimmed and gilded.

Location: JM.

Publication: Listed in *Athenæum,* no. 935 (27 September 1845), 942. Price: 2s. 6d.

Note one: A four-color illuminated wrapper is a cancel at leaf A₁ (see illustration).

Note two: An unbound set of sheets was sent to Fuller early the next year. This copy, now bound in calf, is inscribed by Fuller 'S.M. Fuller | sent her by Mr Delf, | bound for her use | by Mr McElrath, | N.Y. Jany 1846.' (JM).

A 5.1E.b
English edition, second printing: London: George Slater, 1850.

Signature marks and advertisements for Clarke publications are not present. Brown illustrated boards. Price: 1s.

Location: LU (spine repaired).

Illuminated cancel wrapper for A 5.1E.a

A 6.1.a
First edition, first printing (1846)

PAPERS

ON

LITERATURE AND ART.

BY

S. MARGARET FULLER,

AUTHOR OF "A SUMMER ON THE LAKES;" "WOMAN IN THE NINETEENTH
CENTURY," ETC., ETC.

PART II.

NEW YORK:
WILEY AND PUTNAM, 161 BROADWAY.

1846.

A 6.1.a¹: 7³/₈″ × 5″

Two states within the first printing have been noted.

FIRST STATE   SECOND STATE

II.141.17   gazers'   [gazer's

Four issues have been noted.

A 6.1.a¹
First issue

I: [i–v] vi–viii [1] 2–8 [9–11] 12–14 [15] 16–34 [35] 36–42 [43] 44–57 [58] 59–99 [100] 101–150 [151] 152–164 [165–168]

II: [i–viii] [1] 2–21 [22] 23–30 [31] 32–45 [46] 47–107 [108] 109–121 [122] 123–165 [166] 167–175 [176–177] 178–183 [184–188]

I: [1]⁴ 2–8¹²

II: [a]⁴ 1–7¹² 9⁶ 10²

Contents: I: p. i: 'WILEY AND PUTNAM'S | LIBRARY OF | AMERICAN BOOKS. | [rule] | PAPERS ON LITERATURE AND ART. | PART I.'; p. ii: blank; p. iii: title page; p. iv: '[rule] | Entered according to Act of Congress, in the year 1846, by | WILEY AND PUTNAM, | In the Clerk's Office of the District Court of the United States for the | Southern District of New York. | [rule] | [rule] [space] [rule] | R. CRAIGHEAD'S POWER PRESS, [space] T. B. SMITH, STEREOTYPER, | 112 FULTON STREET [space] 216 WILLIAM STREET.'; pp. v–viii: 'PREFACE.' signed 'S. M. F. | *New York, July,* 1846.'; pp. 1–8: 'A Short Essay on Critics'; p. 9: 'CRITICISM ON ENGLISH LITERA-TURE.'; p. 10: blank; pp. 11–14: 'A Dialogue. Poet. Critic.'; pp. 15–34: 'The Two Herberts'; pp. 35–42: 'The Prose Works of Milton'; pp. 43–57: 'The Life of Sir James Mackintosh'; pp. 58–99: 'Modern British Poets'; pp. 100–150: 'The Modern Drama'; pp. 151–164: 'Dialogue'; pp. 165–168: advertisements.

II: p. i: half title (same as I.i); p. ii: blank; p. iii: title page; p. iv: copyright page (same as I.iv); p. v: contents for Part I; p. vi: blank; p. vii: contents for Part II; p. viii: blank; pp. 1–21: 'Poets of the People'; pp. 22–30: 'Miss Barrett's Poems'; pp. 31–45: 'Browning's Poems'; pp. 46–107: 'Lives of the Great Composers; Haydn, Mozart, Handel, Bach, Beethoven'; pp. 108–121: 'A Record of Impressions Produced by the Exhibition of Mr. Allston's Pictures in the Summer of 1839'; pp. 122–159: 'American Literature; Its Position in the Present Time, and Prospects for the Future'; pp. 160–165: 'Swedenborgianism'; pp. 166–175: 'Methodism at the Fountain'; p. 176: blank; pp. 177–183: 'Appendix. The Tragedy of Witchcraft'; p. 184: blank; pp. 185–188: advertisements.

Typography and paper: 7³/₈″ × 5″; wove paper; 33 lines per page. Running heads: *I:* rectos: p. vii: 'PREFACE.'; pp. 3–163: titles of selections; versos: pp. vi–viii: 'PRE-FACE.'; pp. 2–164: 'PAPERS ON LITERATURE AND ART.'. *II:* rectos: pp. 3–175: titles of selections; pp. 179–183: 'APPENDIX.'; versos: pp. 2–174: 'PAPERS ON LITERA-TURE AND ART.'; pp. 178–182: 'APPENDIX.'.

Binding: Light tan paper wrappers with black printing. All within triple-ruled border: front wrapper, recto: '[four lines extracted from an address from the American Copy-right Club] | [rule] | WILEY AND PUTNAM'S | LIBRARY OF AMERICAN BOOKS. | [rule] | No. XIX. [XX.] | [rule] | PAPERS | ON | LITERATURE AND ART. | BY | S. MARGARET FULLER. | IN TWO PARTS—PART I. [II.] | [rule] | NEW YORK AND LONDON. | WILEY AND PUTNAM, 161 BROADWAY: 6 WATERLOO PLACE. | *Price, Fifty Cents.*'. Front wrapper, verso: ads for nos. I–V in Library of American Books series. Back wrapper, recto: ads for nos. VI–X in series. Back wrapper, verso: list of all 20 numbers in series. All edges trimmed.

WILEY AND PUTNAM'S

LIBRARY OF AMERICAN BOOKS.

NO. XIX.

PAPERS

ON

LITERATURE AND ART.

BY

S. MARGARET FULLER.

IN TWO PARTS—PART I.

NEW YORK AND LONDON.

WILEY AND PUTNAM, 161 BROADWAY: 6 WATERLOO PLACE.

Price, Fifty Cents.

Printed paper wrapper for A 6.1.a¹

Location: ViU (2nd state).

Publication: Announced as "about to make . . . appearance" in *Wiley & Putnam's Literary News-Letter,* July 1846, p. 50; as "will be published within the month," August 1846, p. 58; as "To be published in September," September 1846, p. 69. Announced as "may be expected shortly" in *Graham's Magazine,* 29 (September 1846), 156. Reviewed in *United States Magazine and Democratic Review,* 19 (September 1846), 198–202; *Albion,* 12 September 1846, p. 444; *New-York Daily Tribune,* 12 September 1846, p. 2. Price: 50¢ per part.

Note one: A numbering error has resulted in no signature numbered '8'.

Note two: The running head at II, 165, 'AMERICAN LITERATURE.', is incorrect.

Note three: Fuller received 12 percent of the retail price on all copies sold after the publisher's expenses had been made (Fuller to Richard Fuller, n.d., MH).

A 6.1.a²
Second issue: English issue of American sheets

PAPERS

ON

LITERATURE AND ART.

BY

S. MARGARET FULLER,

AUTHOR OF "A SUMMER ON THE LAKES;" "WOMAN IN THE NINETEENTH
CENTURY," ETC. ETC.

PART I.

LONDON:

WILEY & PUTNAM, 6, WATERLOO PLACE.

1846.

[ENTERED AT STATIONERS' HALL.]

A 6.1.a²: 7⁷/₁₆″ × 5³/₁₆″

Two volumes. Untrimmed American sheets with cancel title page; advertisements have been canceled in Part I and omitted in Part II.

Binding: Light green FL cloth (dotted-line-ribbed). Front and back covers: blind-stamped border of ornate leaf and strapwork design with $2^3/4''$ ornament in center. Spine: goldstamped 'PAPERS | ON | LITERATURE | AND ART | [rule] | PART I. [II.]'. Light yellow endpapers.

Locations: 1st state: BC, BE, BO, VtWinoS; 2nd state: MdBJ, MiRochOU.

Publication: Advertised in *Athenæum,* no. 985 (12 September 1846), 942, and *Literary Gazette,* 30 (12 September 1846), 799. Listed as published between 28 August and 14 September in *Publishers' Circular and Booksellers' Record,* 9 (15 September 1846), 266. Price: 3s. 6d. per volume.

A 6.1.a³
Third issue: New York: Wiley and Putnam, 1846.

Two volumes in one. This format results in the following changes: leafs $8_{11,12}$ are canceled; contents pages are redistributed, each being placed before the text of its respective part; advertisements in Part I are omitted; advertisements in Part II remain at the end, are omitted, or are reinserted after Part I. Collation is affected accordingly.

Typography and paper: $7^7/16'' \times 5''$.

Binding: S cloth (fine-ribbed); color variations listed below. Front and back covers: blindstamped triple-ruled border with a triangular design midway on each side, a square strapwork design in each corner, and a strapwork design surrounding a circle in the center. Spine: blindstamped rules with goldstamped 'LIBRARY | OF | AMERI-CAN | BOOKS | PAPERS ON | LITERATURE | AND ART | [rule] | S. M. FULLER | WILEY & PUTNAM'. Flyleaves. Endpaper variations listed below.

1. Brown cloth; brown star and dot design on white endpapers.
   Locations: CaOWtU, JM, MA, OHi, VtMiM (2nd state).
2. Dark gray blue cloth; blue star and dot design on white endpapers.
   Locations: CtHT-W, MWiW, N, OCl, TU (1st state).
3. Purple cloth; brown star and dot design on white endpapers.
   Location: NN (2nd state).

Publication: Apparently published at the same time as the first issue. Price: $1.25. Inscribed copies: CaOWtU (19 September 1846), MA (November 1846).

Note one: A copy in a later binding has been noted: brown cloth (diagonal-ribbed), with blindstamped 'Putnam's Choice Library' inside a four-leaf-clover design at bottom of spine and brown star and dot design on white endpapers: MWA (2nd state).

Note two: A copy in a later binding has been noted: light green S cloth (fine diagonal-ribbed), with blindstamped single-ruled border with 'Putnam's Choice Library' inside $3^3/4''$ ornament in center on front and back covers; spine: blindstamped rules with goldstamped 'PAPERS | ON | LITERATURE | AND | ART | [rule] | FULLER'; brown star and dot design on white endpapers: MWA (2nd state).

Note three: A copy in a later binding has been noted: same as in Note two, except it has blindstamped 'Putnam's Choice Library' inside a four-leaf-clover design at bottom of spine and buff endpapers: CaNBFU (1st state).

A 6.1.a⁴
Fourth issue: London: Wiley & Putnam, 1846.

Two volumes in one. Untrimmed American sheets with cancel title page; advertisements have been canceled in Part I and omitted in Part II.

Binding: Light green FL cloth (dotted-line-ribbed). Front and back covers: blind-stamped border of small leaf design. Spine: blindstamped rules with goldstamped 'PAPERS | ON | LITERATURE'. Cream endpapers.

Location: JM.

A 6.1.b
Second printing: New York: Wiley and Putnam, 1848.

Two volumes in one.

Binding: S cloth (fine diagonal-ribbed); color variations listed below. Front and back covers: blindstamped triple-ruled border with triangular design midway on each side, square strapwork design in each corner, and 'Library of Choice Reading' inside 3¹/₂″ ornament in center. Spine: goldstamped 'FULLER'S | PAPERS | ON | LITERATURE | AND ART' and blindstamped 'Library of Choice Reading' inside a four-leaf-clover design at bottom; variations listed below. Light yellow endpapers.

1. Light green cloth; spine: blindstamped leafy-spray and filigree design.
   Location: IU.
2. Medium purple blue cloth; spine: blindstamped leafy-spray and filigree design.
   Location: NhD.
3. Medium blue purple cloth; spine: blindstamped rules.
   Locations: CaBViV, TxFTC.

Note: All copies examined (including rebound copies at NmU, OCIW) read 'gazer's' at II.141.17, as do subsequent printings and editions.

A 6.1.c
Third printing (1852)

LITERATURE AND ART.

BY S. MARGARET FULLER,

AUTHOR OF A SUMMER ON THE LAKES, WOMAN IN THE NINETEENTH CENTURY, ETC., ETC.

Two Parts, in One Volume.

CONTAINING:

With an Introduction,

BY HORACE GREELEY.

NEW YORK:

PUBLISHED BY FOWLERS AND WELLS,

CLINTON HALL, 131 NASSAU STREET.

Boston, 142 Washington-St.]   1852.   [London, No. 142 Strand.

A 6.1.c: $7^{7}/_{16}'' \times 4^{11}/_{16}''$

[i–ii] [i] ii–iv [v]; all else same as in the first printing (see A6.1.a³).

[1–15]¹²

Contents: p. i: title page; p. ii: blank; pp. i–iv: 'INTRODUCTION' signed 'H. G.' [Horace Greeley], dated 'NEW YORK, *May 1st,* 1852.'; pp. v–viii: 'PREFACE.'; pp. 1–164: text; p. i: 'LITERATURE AND ART. | PART II.'; p. ii: blank; pp. 1–183: text; p. 184: blank.

Typography and paper: 7⁷/₁₆″ × 4¹¹/₁₆″; wove paper; 33 lines per page. Running heads: same as in first printing, except: recto: p. iii: 'INTRODUCTION.'; versos: pp. ii–iv: 'INTRODUCTION.'.

Binding: C cloth (coarse sand-grained); color variations listed below. Front and back covers: blindstamped triple-ruled border with ornamental design in each corner and 3¹/₂″ ornament in center. Spine: blindstamped rules with goldstamped 'LITERATURE | AND | ART | [rule] | S. MARGARET FULLER | NEW-YORK. | FOWLERS & WELLS'. Flyleaves. Light green endpapers. All edges trimmed.

1. Black cloth.
   Locations: CaOLU, CtU, DGU, DLC, IaU, JM, MA, MeBa, NBC, NbKS, NbL, NcD, NhHi, OKentU, OrFP, OrU, WBB.
2. Brown cloth.
   Locations: CCC, JM, MWA, MdU, MeU, NBronSL, OYesA, TxDaM.
3. Green cloth.
   Location: NPV.
4. Medium purple blue cloth.
   Locations: JM, MnU, NGcU, NRU, NhM, WaPU.

Publication: Announced as "in press" and "will be published on the 1st of July" in *American Phrenological Journal,* 15 (March 1852), 71. Listed as published between 15 May and 1 June in *Literary World,* 10 (10 July 1852), 31. Price: $1.00. Inscribed copy: OKentU (August 1852).

Note: Copies with advertisements on pp. [185]–[188] have been noted: CtU, IaU, JM (brown), MdU, MeBa, MnU, NBronSL, NbL, NcD, OKentU.

A6.1.d
Fourth printing: New York: AMS Press, 1972.

Facsimile of the second issue.

A 6.2.a
Second edition, first printing (1860)

ART, LITERATURE,

AND

THE DRAMA.

BY

MARGARET FULLER OSSOLI,

AUTHOR OF "AT HOME AND ABROAD, " WOMAN IN THE NINETEENTH CENTURY," "LIFE WITHOUT AND LIFE WITHIN," ETC.

EDITED BY HER BROTHER,

ARTHUR B. FULLER.

———————

BOSTON:
BROWN, TAGGARD AND CHASE.
NEW YORK: SHELDON & CO. PHILADELPHIA: J. B. LIPPINCOTT & CO.
LONDON: SAMPSON LOW, SON & CO.
1860.

A 6.2.a: 7⁹/₁₆″ × 4³/₄″

[1–2] 3–9 [10] 11 [12] 13–175 [176] 177–351 [352] 353 [354] 355–449 [450–452]

[1]–37⁶ 38⁴

Contents: p. 1: title page; p. 2: 'Entered, according to Act of Congress, in the year 1859, by | ARTHUR B. FULLER, | In the Clerk's Office of the District Court of the District of Massachusetts.'; pp. 3–4: 'PREFACE, BY THE EDITOR.' dated 'WATER-TOWN, MASS., 1859'; pp. 5–8: 'PREFACE.'; p. 9: contents; p. 10: blank; p. 11: 'PART I. | ART AND LITERATURE.'; p. 12: blank; pp. 13–174: text, Part I of *Papers on Literature and Art;* p. 175: 'PART II. | ART AND LITERATURE.'; p. 176: blank; pp. 177–351: text, Part II of *Papers on Literature and Art,* except for "Appendix. The Tragedy of Witchcraft"; p. 352: blank; p. 353: 'PART III. | THE DRAMA.'; p. 354: blank; pp. 355–357: 'PREFACE BY THE TRANSLATOR.'; p. 358: 'DRAMATIS PERSONAE.'; pp. 359–449: 'The Drama of Torquato Tasso'; pp. 450–452: blank.

Typography and paper: 7⁹/₁₆″ × 4³/₄″; wove paper; 33 lines per page. Running heads: rectos: p. 7: 'PREFACE.'; pp. 15–351: titles of selections; p. 357: 'PREFACE BY THE TRANSLATOR.'; pp. 361–449: 'TORQUATO TASSO.'; versos: pp. 4–8: 'PREFACE.'; pp. 14–350: 'PAPERS ON LITERATURE AND ART.'; p. 356: 'PREFACE BY THE TRANSLATOR.'; pp. 360–448: 'THE DRAMA OF'.

Binding: Black S cloth (fine-ribbed). Front and back covers: blindstamped triple-ruled border with 3³/₄″ ornament in center. Spine: blindstamped bands and single filigree design with goldstamped 'MARGARET | FULLER'S | WORKS | [rule] | ART | LITERATURE | AND THE | DRAMA | BROWN, TAGGARD & CHASE'. Flyleaves. Yellow endpapers. All edges trimmed.

Locations: CSmH, CaOTY, IEN, MA, MiBsA.

Publication: Announced as to be published "soon" in *Bookseller's Medium and Publisher's Circular,* 15 October 1859, p. 98. Advertised as "Ready in a Few Days" in *Bookseller's Medium and Publisher's Circular,* 16 January 1860, p. 218, and 1 February 1860, p. 244. Advertised as "Ready in a Few Days" in *Boston Daily Evening Transcript,* 9 January 1860, p. 3, and *Boston Daily Advertiser,* 11 January 1860, p. 2. Inscribed copy: CaOTY (5 September 1860).

Note: The running head at p. 341, 'AMERICAN LITERATURE.', is incorrect.

A 6.2.b
Second printing: New York: The Tribune Association, 1869.

[1–18¹² 19⁶ 20⁴]

Binding: L cloth (morocco); color variations listed below. Front and back covers: blindstamped single-ruled border with 2⁷/₈″ ornament in center. Spine: goldstamped '[ornamental band] | ART, | LITERATURE, | AND THE | DRAMA. | MARGARET | FULLER | OSSOLI. | TRIBUNE | [ornamental band]'. Flyleaves. Green endpapers. All edges trimmed.

1. Dark brown cloth.
   Locations: ABH, NbL, OAkU, OCl, OClW, PHC, RWe, TxDN.
2. Dark reddish orange cloth.
   Locations: In, JM, MU, MnHi.
3. Green cloth.
   Locations: MH, NjNbS.
4. Medium purple cloth.
   Locations: IP, MWalB, MiU, NNMer, NSyU, OMC, VtSjA.

Publication: Price: six-volume Tribune edition of Fuller's works, $10.00 per set. Inscribed copy: NbL (1 September 1869).

Note: Leaf 20₄ is canceled.

A 6.2.c
Third printing: Boston: Roberts Brothers, 1874.

[1–20¹²]

Binding: L cloth (morocco); color variations listed below. Front and back covers: blindstamped double band with perpendicular lines. Spine: blindstamped bands with goldstamped 'MARGARET | FULLER'S | WORKS | [ornamental rule] | ART, | LITERATURE, | THE DRAMA. | [ornamental rule] | R [star-like publisher's device] B'. Flyleaves. Brown endpapers. All edges trimmed.

1. Dark green cloth.
   Locations: CLSU, MWC, MdBP, MoKiT.
2. Dark reddish brown cloth.
   Location: BL.
3. Dark reddish orange cloth.
   Locations: FTaSU, JM, LNHT, MeBa, NBuU, OCU, TxDW, WMU, WU.
4. Dark reddish purple cloth.
   Location: MWA.

Publication: According to the Roberts Brothers' cost books, 280 copies were printed and bound as of 1 February 1874. Mrs. Arthur B. Fuller retained the plates and received 10 percent on the retail price of each copy sold. Price: $1.50. Inscribed copy: NBu [rebound] (April 1874).

SUBSEQUENT PRINTINGS

A 6.2.d
Fourth printing: Boston: Roberts Brothers, 1875.

According to the Roberts Brothers' cost books, 240 copies were printed between 24 February and 14 April 1875. Price: $1.50.

A 6.2.e
Fifth printing: Boston: Roberts Brothers, 1889.

According to the Roberts Brothers' cost books, 280 copies were printed as of 6 December 1889. A second issue, with the sheets of this printing (with the Roberts Brothers title page) bound in Little, Brown and Company casings, has been noted.

A 7 MEMOIRS OF MARGARET FULLER OSSOLI

A 7.1.a
First edition, first printing (1852)

MEMOIRS

OF

MARGARET FULLER OSSOLI.

VOL. I.

Only a learned and a manly soul
  I purposed her, that should with even powers
The rock, the spindle, and the shears control
  Of Destiny, and spin her own free hours.
                                    BEN JONSON.

Però che ogni diletto nostro e doglia
Sta in sì e nò saper, voler, potere ;
Adunque quel sol può, che col dovere
Ne trae la ragion fuor di sua soglia.

Adunque tu, lettor di queste note,
S' a te vuoi esser buono, e agli altri caro,
Vogli sempre poter quel che tu debbi.
                              LEONARDO DA VINCI.

BOSTON:
PHILLIPS, SAMPSON AND COMPANY.
M DCCC LII.

A 7.1.a: 7⁵/₈″ × 4⁷/₈″

I: [v–vii] viii [9–11] 12–57 [58–61] 62–71 [72] 73–101 [102] 103–111 [112] 113–130 [131] 132–142 [143–145] 146–198 [199–201] 202–316 [317–319] 320–351 [352]

II: [i–iv] [i] ii [3–5] 6–116 [117–119] 120–168 [169–171] 172–330 [331–333] 334–352

I: [1¹⁰ 2–14¹² 15⁸]

II: [1² 2–15¹² 16⁸]

Contents: I: p. v: title page; p. vi: 'Entered according to Act of Congress, in the year 1851, | BY R. F. FULLER, | In the Clerk's Office of the District Court of the District of Massachusetts. | Stereotyped by | HOBART & ROBBINS; | NEW ENGLAND TYPE AND STEREOTYPE FOUNDRY, | BOSTON.'; pp. vii–viii: contents for vol. I; p. 9: 'YOUTH. | AUTOBIOGRAPHY. | [rule] | [2 lines of German verse] | GOETHE. | [2 lines of verse] | TENNYSON. | [8 lines of German verse] | SCHILLER.'; p. 10: '[9 lines of verse] | SHELLEY. | [5 lines of verse] | BROWNING.'; pp. 11–57: 'I. Youth.'; p. 58: blank; p. 59: 'LIFE IN CAMBRIDGE. | BY JAMES FREEMAN CLARKE. | [rule] | "Extraordinary, generous seeking." | GOETHE. | [4 lines of verse] | THEODORE KOERNER. | [6 lines of verse] | SHELLEY.'; p. 60: 17-line quotation from "Dichtung und Wahrheit," *North American Review,* January 1817; pp. 61–142: 'II. Cambridge.'; p. 143: 'GROTON AND PROVIDENCE. | LETTERS AND JOURNALS. | [rule] | [4 lines of verse] | HERBERT. | [5 lines of prose] | FICHTE.'; p. 144: '[8 lines of verse] | ELIZABETH B. BARRETT. | [8 lines of verse] | BROWNING.'; pp. 145–198: 'III. Groton and Providence.'; p. 199: 'VISITS TO CONCORD. | [rule] | BY R. W. EMERSON.'; p. 200: 'EXTRACT FROM A LETTER FROM MADAME ARCONATI TO R. W. EMERSON. | [4 lines in French]'; pp. 201–316: 'IV. Visits to Concord.'; p. 317: 'CONVERSATIONS IN BOSTON. | BY R. W. EMERSON. | [rule] | "Do not scold me; they are guests of my eyes. Do not frown,—they | want no bread; they are guests of my words." | TARTAR ECLOGUES.'; p. 318: blank; pp. 319–351: 'V. Conversations in Boston.'; p. 352: blank.

II: pp. i–ii: blank; p. iii: title page (same as I.v); p. iv: copyright page (same as I.vi); pp. i–ii: contents for vol. II; p. 3: 'JAMAICA PLAIN. | BY W. H. CHANNING. | [rule] | [9 lines of Italian verse] | DANTE. | [8 lines of German verse] | GOETHE.'; p. 4: '[5 lines of verse] | TENNYSON. | [3 lines of prose] | LANDOR. | [8 lines of verse] | ELIZABETH BARRETT.'; pp. 5–116: 'VI. Jamaica Plain.'; p. 117: 'NEW YORK. | JOURNALS, LETTERS, &c. | [rule] | [8 lines of unattributed verse (from George Herbert)] | [3 lines of Italian verse] | ALFIERI. | [6 lines of verse] | TAYLOR.'; p. 118: '[12 lines of verse] | SHAKSPEARE. [Sonnet lxxiii.] | [6 lines of German verse] | SCHILLER. | [9 lines of verse] | TENNYSON.'; pp. 119–168: 'VII. New York.'; p. 169: 'EUROPE. | LETTERS. | [rule] | [4 lines of verse] | BROWNING. | [7 lines of verse] | WORDSWORTH. | [5 lines of Italian verse] | FILICAJA.'; p. 170: '[6 lines of verse] | BROWNING. | [6 lines of verse] | LANDOR. | [4 lines of verse] | STERLING.'; pp. 171–330: 'VIII. Europe.'; p. 331: 'HOMEWARD. | [rule] | [8 lines of verse] | BROWNING. | [5 lines of verse] | ELIZABETH BARRETT.'; p. 332: '[15 lines of Italian verse] | DANTE. | [6 lines of Italian verse] | PETRARCA.'; pp. 333–352: 'IX. Homeward.'.

Typography and paper: 7⁵/₈" × 4⁷/₈"; wove paper; 33 lines per page. Running heads: *I:* rectos: p. 13: 'SISTER'S DEATH.'; p. 15: 'OVERWORK.'; p. 17: 'STUDIES.'; p. 19: 'ROME.'; p. 21: 'GODS OF GREECE.'; p. 23: 'GARDEN.'; p. 25: 'LIBRARY.'; p. 27: 'SHAKSPEARE.'; p. 29: 'CERVANTES.'; p. 31: 'READING.'; p. 33: 'FIRST FRIEND.'; p. 35: 'INTERCOURSE.'; p. 37: 'RELATIONS.'; p. 39: 'PARTING.'; p. 41: 'CHILDREN.'; p. 43: 'EXCITEMENTS.'; p. 45: 'BRIGHT MOOD.'; p. 47: 'ANGUISH.'; p. 49: 'TRIAL.'; p. 51: 'PENITENCE.'; p. 53: 'INDUSTRY.'; p. 55: 'STUDIES.'; p. 57: 'TRUE LIFE.'; p. 63: 'COUSINSHIP.'; p. 65: 'CHARACTER.'; p. 67: 'GENEROSITY.'; p. 69: 'GENIUS.'; p. 71: 'TOPICS.'; p. 73: 'CONFIDENCE.'; p. 75: 'INSIGHT.'; p. 77: 'CONSTANCY.'; p. 79: 'TRUTH.';

p. 81: 'OPENNESS.'; p. 83: 'DISCERNMENT.'; p. 85: 'CIRCUMSTANCES.'; pp. 87–89: 'COMPANIONS.'; p. 91: 'APPEARANCE.'; p. 93: 'ROMANCE.'; p. 95: 'CONVERSA-TION.'; p. 97: 'EUPHORION.'; p. 99: 'LONELINESS.'; p. 101: 'HONOR.'; p. 103: 'SO-CIAL INTERCOURSE.'; pp. 105–109: 'CONVERSATION.'; p. 111: 'PASSION-FLOWER.'; p. 113: 'GENIUS.'; p. 115: 'CRITICISM.'; p. 117: 'OTTILIA.'; p. 119: 'NOVALIS.'; p. 121: 'LESSING.'; p. 123: 'PHILOSOPHY.'; p. 125: 'ELOQUENCE.'; p. 127: 'FICHTE.'; p. 129: 'GOETHE.'; pp. 133–137: 'AIMS AND IDEAS.'; pp. 139–141: 'THANKSGIVING.'; p. 147: 'RICHTER.'; p. 149: 'AMERICAN HISTORY.'; p. 151: 'MISS MARTINEAU.'; p. 153: 'IN-TELLECTUAL GUIDE.'; p. 155: 'DEATH OF HER FATHER.'; p. 157: 'PERPLEXITIES.'; p. 159: 'TRIAL.'; pp. 161–163: 'DEATH IN LIFE.'; p. 165: 'MACKINTOSH.'; p. 167: 'WIL-HELM MEISTER.'; p. 169: 'TIECK.'; p. 171: 'A. B. ALCOTT.'; p. 173: 'WINTER'S WORK.'; p. 175: 'DR. CHANNING.'; p. 177: 'SCHOOL EXPERIENCES.'; p. 179: 'LAST WORDS.'; p. 181: 'JOHN NEAL.'; p. 183: 'J. J. GURNEY.'; p. 185: 'R. H. DANA.'; p. 187: 'FANNY KEMBLE.'; p. 189: 'POWER OF ART.'; p. 191: 'MAGNANIMITY.'; p. 193: 'JUSTICE.'; p. 195: 'VOCATIONS.'; p. 197: 'COMMUNION.'; p. 203: 'CONCORD.'; pp. 205–213: 'FRIENDS.'; pp. 215–217: 'CONVERSATION.'; pp. 219–221: 'ARCANA.'; pp. 223–225: 'DÆMONOLOGY.'; pp. 227–233: 'TEMPERAMENT.'; pp. 235–237: 'SELF-ESTEEM.'; pp. 239–243: 'BOOKS.'; pp. 245–261: 'CRITICISM.'; p. 263: 'NATURE.'; pp. 265–277: 'ART.'; p. 279: 'LETTERS.'; pp. 281–289: 'FRIENDSHIP.'; pp. 291–293: 'PROBLEMS OF LIFE.'; pp. 295–297: 'WOMAN, OR ARTIST?'; pp. 299–301: 'HEROISM.'; pp. 303–307: 'TRUTH.'; p. 309: 'ECSTACY.'; pp. 311–315: 'CONVERSATION.'; p. 321: 'BOSTON.'; p. 323: 'THE DIAL.'; pp. 325–339: 'CONVERSATIONS.'; p. 341: 'FINE ARTS.'; pp. 343–349: 'CONVERSATIONS.'; p. 351: 'FAREWELLS.'; versos: p. viii: 'TABLE OF CON-TENTS.'; pp. 12–56: 'YOUTH.'; pp. 62–142: 'CAMBRIDGE.'; pp. 146–198: 'GROTON AND PROVIDENCE.'; pp. 202–316: 'VISITS TO CONCORD.'; pp. 320–322: 'CONVER-SATIONS IN BOSTON.'; pp. 324–350: 'BOSTON.'.

II: p. 7: 'FIRST IMPRESSIONS.'; pp. 9–11: 'A CLUE.'; p. 13: 'THE TRANSCENDEN-TALIST.'; pp. 15–17: ' "THOSE MEN." '; p. 19: 'GENIUS.'; p. 21: 'RARE TRAITS.'; p. 23: 'PENETRATION.'; p. 25: 'THE DIAL.'; p. 27: 'NEW ENGLAND.'; p. 29: 'UTOPIA.'; p. 31: 'A SUMMER-DAY.'; p. 33: 'MYTHOLOGY.'; p. 35: 'TEMPERAMENT.'; p. 37: 'TRAGEDY.'; p. 39: 'THE FRIEND.'; p. 41: 'FRIENDSHIP.'; p. 43: 'CHIVALRY.'; p. 45: 'RIVER-LIFE.'; p. 47: 'COMPENSATIONS.'; p. 49: 'YUCA FILAMENTOSA.'; p. 51: 'TRAGEDY.'; p. 53: 'ANGEL MINISTRY.'; p. 55: 'MELISSA.'; p. 57: 'COMMUNITY.'; p. 59: 'NEWPORT.'; p. 61: 'MOONLIGHT.'; p. 63: 'CHILDREN.'; p. 65: 'EXPERIENCE.'; p. 67: 'CONCORD.'; p. 69: 'DR. CHANNING.'; p. 71: 'TRUE INTERCOURSE.'; p. 73: 'SOCIALISM.'; p. 75: 'BROOK FARM.'; p. 77: 'INTELLECT.'; p. 79: 'INFLUENCE.'; p. 81: 'CREDO.'; p. 83: 'COMMUNION.'; p. 85: 'UNITARIANISM.'; p. 87: 'SOCRATES.'; p. 89: 'MAN.'; p. 91: 'JESUS CHRIST.'; p. 93: 'TRANSFORMATION.'; p. 95: 'RAPTURE.'; p. 97: 'BEAUTY.'; p. 99: 'ILLUMINATION.'; p. 101: 'RENUNCIATION.'; p. 103: 'CONTRASTS.'; p. 105: 'PER-PLEXITY.'; p. 107: 'PRAYER.'; p. 109: 'HUMILITY.'; p. 111: 'ARROGANCE.'; p. 113: 'INFLUENCE.'; p. 115: 'SUB ROSA CRUX.'; p. 121: 'FAMILY.'; p. 123: 'THE DAUGH-TER.'; p. 125: 'THE SISTER.'; p. 127: 'COUNSEL.'; p. 129: 'RELIGION.'; p. 131: 'HOPES AND PLANS.'; p. 133: 'MOUNTAINS.'; p. 135: 'OBSTACLES.'; p. 137: 'READINGS.'; p. 139: 'WOMAN.'; p. 141: 'TEXAS ANNEXATION.'; p. 143: 'TRUE RELATIONS.'; p. 145: 'SING-SING.'; p. 147: 'CHRISTMAS.'; p. 149: 'BLACKWELL'S ISLAND.'; p. 151: 'THE TRIBUNE.'; p. 153: 'HORACE GREELEY.'; p. 155: ' "WOMAN'S RIGHTS." '; p. 157: 'LIBERALITY.'; p. 159: 'INDIGNATION.'; p. 161: 'LOVE OF CHILDREN.'; p. 163: 'WRIT-INGS.'; p. 165: 'SOCIETY.'; p. 167: 'JUSTICE.'; pp. 173–175: 'WORDSWORTH.'; p. 177: 'EDINBURGH.'; p. 179: 'A NIGHT ON BEN LOMOND.'; p. 181: 'BEN LOMOND.'; p. 183: 'LONDON.'; pp. 185–189: 'CARLYLE.'; p. 191: 'PARIS.'; pp. 193–197: 'GEORGE SAND.'; p. 199: 'RACHEL.'; pp. 201–207: 'PARIS.'; p. 209: 'ROME.'; pp. 211–213: 'MILAN.'; pp. 215–217: 'THE LAKES.'; p. 219: 'FLORENCE.'; pp. 221–225: 'ROME.'; p. 227: 'AMERICANS IN ITALY.'; pp. 229–239: 'ROME.'; pp. 241–243: 'RIETI.'; pp. 245–

267: 'ROME.'; p. 269: 'RIETI.'; pp. 271–279: 'THE WIFE AND MOTHER.'; pp. 281–291: 'PRIVATE MARRIAGE.'; pp. 293–295: 'AQUILA AND RIETI.'; pp. 297–301: 'RIETI.'; p. 303: 'CALM AFTER STORM.'; pp. 305–329: 'FLORENCE.'; pp. 335–337: 'OMENS.'; p. 339: 'THE VOYAGE.'; pp. 341–351: 'THE WRECK.'; versos: p. ii: 'TABLE OF CONTENTS.'; pp. 6–116: 'JAMAICA PLAIN.'; pp. 120–168: 'NEW YORK.'; pp. 172–330: 'EUROPE.'; pp. 334–352: 'HOMEWARD.'.

Binding: Black S cloth (fine-ribbed). Front and back covers: blindstamped single-ruled border with a design inside each corner (variations listed below) and 3³/₄" ornament in center. Spine: blindstamped rules and boxes with goldstamped 'MEMOIRS | OF | MARGARET FULLER | OSSOLI | [rule] | VOL. I. [II.]'; variations listed below. Flyleaves. Pale yellow endpapers. All edges trimmed.

1. Covers: three double ring-like ornaments; spine: 'MARGARET FULLER | OSSOLI' in ³/₁₆" type.
   Locations: CaBViV, IaU (II), JM (I), MNt, MWH (I), MiU, OKentU, OMC, ScGF (II), UPB, VtMiM (II).
2. Covers: three double ring-like ornaments; spine: 'MARGARET FULLER | OSSOLI' in ¹/₈" type.
   Locations: JM, LNHT, MH, MNa, MeB, NNPM, Nh (II), OkU (I), ViU, VtMiM (I), VtMiM.
3. Covers: ornamental filigree design; spine: 'MARGARET FULLER | OSSOLI' in ¹/₈" type.
   Location: MsHaU.
4. Covers: crescent design; spine: 'MARGARET FULLER | OSSOLI' in ³/₁₆" type.
   Location: RNR.

Publication: Phillips, Sampson wrote Emerson on 23 September 1851 to mention that all the copy had not yet been sent and that the stereotypers were "driven" trying to get the *Memoirs* out in time for the Christmas trade (MH). W. H. Channing wrote on 20 November 1851: "I am just finishing the last chapter of Margaret Ossoli's Memoir & cannot budge an inch till that is forwarded to the printer" (Madeleine B. Stern, "William Henry Channing's Letters on 'Woman in her Social Relations'," *Cornell Library Journal*, no. 6 [Autumn 1968], 60). Advertised as "Will soon publish" in *Literary World*, 10 (3 January 1852), 18, and as "Just Published," 10 (14 February 1852), 127. Advertised as "This day published" in *Boston Daily Advertiser*, 16 February 1852, p. 4. Listed as published between 14 February and 6 March in *Literary World*, 10 (13 March 1852), 193. Price: $2.00 per set. Inscribed copies: NNPM (25 February 1852), OKentU [rebound] (March 1852), JM (4 March 1852).

Note one: Copies with advertisements for Phillips, Sampson publications have been noted:

1. [I, 353–360]: CaBViV, JM, LNHT, MH, MWH, MsHaU, OkU, VtMiM.
2. Four pages present before title page of vol I and [I, 353–360]: MH, NNPM, OKentU.
3. Four pages present before title page of vol. II: CaBViV, NNPM.

Note two: New York Home Journal (13 March 1852), p. 3, stated: "The first thousand of Emerson and Channing's 'Life of Margaret Fuller' was sold in twenty-four hours." According to J. F. Clarke, "a second and third edition were hurried through the press, and there seemed every prospect of a wide popularity to the book, when, *presto*, the sale stopped. Nor has it ever been renewed." The reason, according to Clarke, was that Phillips, Sampson's presses were tied up to meet the demand for copies of another best seller, Stowe's *Uncle Tom's Cabin* (Clarke, *Autobiography, Diary and Correspondence*, ed. Edward Everett Hale [Boston: Houghton, Mifflin, 1891], p. 189).

Note three: The *Memoirs* was edited by Ralph Waldo Emerson, William Henry Channing, and James Freeman Clarke, although this was not acknowledged on the title page until the 1860 printing. The division of labor (according both to the contents pages and to Channing's annotated copy of the *Memoirs* at MiD) was as follows: Emerson: "IV. Visits to Concord." and "V. Conversations in Boston."; Channing: "I. Youth.," "III. Groton and Providence.," "VI. Jamaica Plain.," "VII. New York.," and "IX. Homeward."; Clarke: "II. Cambridge." Emerson and Channing coedited "VIII. Europe.," with Channing "chiefly" doing the work, especially II, 267–330. Channing also wrote in his copy of the *Memoirs:* "The plan of the book,—the division into parts or chapters,—the selection of mottoes,—the filling up of the spaces between the extracts, the interweaving of the whole,—and indeed all parts of it, not specially referred to others, are the work of W.H.C."

Note four: No order of priority has been established for the first three printings.

A 7.1.b
Second printing: Boston: Phillips, Sampson and Company, 1852.

I: [1]⁴ 2–8⁶ 9² 9*⁴ 10–16⁶ 17² 17*⁴ 18–29⁶ 30²

II: [a]² 1–29⁶ 30⁴

Binding: Black S cloth (fine-ribbed). Front and back covers: three double ring-like ornaments inside border at each corner. Spine: blindstamped rules and boxes; variations in goldstamping listed below.

1. 'MARGARET FULLER | OSSOLI' in ³/₁₆″ type.
   Locations: CCC (I), CtW, IDeKN (I), MChB, MCo, MH, MWH (I), MnDuU, NNMan, NNMer (I), OCIW (I), ODaU, RHi (I).
2. 'MARGARET FULLER | OSSOLI' in ¹/₈″ type.
   Locations: CLSU (I), CSmH, IaAS (I), MLen (I), MMeT (I), MeWC (I), MnU, NHC (I), Nh (I), OCIWHi (I), OHi (I), PPA (I), T (I).

Publication: Inscribed copy: MLen (March 1852).

Note: Copies with advertisements for Phillips, Sampson publications have been noted:

1. [I, 353–360]: CLSU, CSmH, IDeKN, IaAS, MH, OCIW, OCIWHi, OHi.
2. [II, 353–356]: CtW, MChB, MCo, MnDuU, MnU, NNMan, ODaU.

A 7.1.c
Third printing: Boston: Phillips, Sampson and Company, 1852.

I: [1]⁴ 2–29⁶ 30²

II: [a]² 1–29⁶ 30²

Binding: Black S cloth (fine-ribbed). Front and back covers: design inside border at each corner; variations listed below. Spine: blindstamped rules and boxes; variations in goldstamping listed below.

1. Covers: three double ring-like ornaments; spine: 'MARGARET FULLER | OSSOLI' in ³/₁₆″ type.
   Locations: CLU (II), CaOLU, IDeKN (II), JM, MLow, NNF, Nh (II), OCIW (II), RHi (II), TU.
2. Covers: three double ring-like ornaments; spine: 'MARGARET FULLER | OSSOLI' in ¹/₈″ type.
   Locations: CLSU (II), CSmH (I), CU-S, ICHi, IaAS (II), MA (II), MLen (II), MMeT (II), MeWC (II), NNS, OCIWHi (II), PPA (II), T (II), TxU, Vi (II).

3. Covers: ornamental filigree design; spine: 'MARGARET FULLER | OSSOLI' in ¹/₈″ type.
   Location: WaPU (II).

Note: A copy of vol. I with advertisements on pp. [353]–[360] for Phillips, Sampson publications has been noted: NNS.

A 7.1.d
Fourth printing: Boston: Phillips, Sampson and Company, 1852.

"VI. Jamaica Plain." and "IX. Homeward." are credited to W. H. Channing in the table of contents to vol. II, and a textual revision is present:

   I.98.19–21 Friendship, with | the following letter, written in 1839, but referring to this | early period: [Friendship with | the two following passages, the second of which was | written to some one unknown to me:

I: [1¹⁰ 2–14¹² 15⁸]

II: [1² 2–15¹² 16⁸]

Binding: Black S cloth (fine-ribbed). Front and back covers: design inside border at each corner; variations listed below. Spine variations listed below.

1. Covers: three double ring-like ornaments; spine: blindstamped rules and boxes, goldstamped 'MARGARET FULLER | OSSOLI' in ³/₁₆″ type.
   Locations: CaNBFU (I), MWC, MiDU (II).
2. Covers: three double ring-like ornaments; spine: blindstamped rules and boxes, goldstamped 'MARGARET FULLER | OSSOLI' in ¹/₈″ type.
   Location: NHC (II).
3. Covers: ornamental filigree design; spine: blindstamped rules and boxes, gold-stamped 'MARGARET FULLER | OSSOLI' in ³/₁₆″ type.
   Location: MsU (I).
4. Covers: ornamental filigree design; spine: blindstamped rules and boxes, gold-stamped 'MARGARET FULLER | OSSOLI' in ¹/₈″ type.
   Locations: CCC (II), CaNBFU (II), JM (II), PSC.
5. Covers: crescent design; spine: blindstamped rules and boxes, goldstamped 'MARGARET FULLER | OSSOLI' in ³/₁₆″ type.
   Locations: BLK, ICIU, JM (I).
6. Covers: crescent design; spine: blindstamped rules and boxes, goldstamped 'MARGARET FULLER | OSSOLI' in ¹/₈″ type.
   Location: TxSmS (II).
7. Covers: ornamental filigree design; spine: blindstamped filigree design, gold-stamped 'MARGARET FULLER | OSSOLI' in ¹/₈″ type.
   Locations: OkU (II), VtNN (II).
8. Covers: sheaf of wheat design; spine: blindstamped filigree design, goldstamped 'MARGARET FULLER | OSSOLI' in ³/₁₆″ type.
   Locations: MH, NhHi.
9. Covers: sheaf of wheat design; spine: blindstamped filigree design, goldstamped 'MARGARET FULLER | OSSOLI' in ¹/₈″ type.
   Location: CaQMM.
10. Covers: intersecting loops design; spine: blindstamped filigree design, gold-stamped 'MARGARET FULLER | OSSOLI' in ³/₁₆″ type.
    Location: MBC.

Note one: Copies of vol. II with advertisements on pp. [353]–[356] have been noted: CCC, CaNBFU, CaQMM, JM, MH, NhHi, PSC.

Note two: All subsequent printings of the American edition have the revised reading at I.98.19–21 and have the W. H. Channing identification in the table of contents to vol. II.

A 7.1.e
Fifth printing: Boston: Phillips, Sampson and Company, 1852.

I: [1]² 2–8⁶ 9² 9*⁴ 10–16⁶ 17² 17*⁴ 18–29⁶ 30²

II: [a]² 1–29⁶ 30²

Binding: Black S cloth (fine-ribbed). Front and back covers: design inside border at each corner; variations listed below. Spine variations listed below.

1. Covers: ornamental filigree design; spine: blindstamped rules and boxes, gold-stamped 'MARGARET FULLER | OSSOLI' in ³/₁₆″ type.
   Locations: FU, MsU (II).
2. Covers: ornamental filigree design; spine: blindstamped rules and boxes, gold-stamped 'MARGARET FULLER | OSSOLI' in ¹/₈″ type.
   Locations: FTaSU, PHi.
3. Covers: three double ring-like ornaments; spine: blindstamped filigree design, goldstamped 'MARGARET FULLER | OSSOLI' in ³/₁₆″ type.
   Location: BMR.
4. Covers: ornamental filigree design; spine: blindstamped filigree design, gold-stamped 'MARGARET FULLER | OSSOLI' in ¹/₈″ type.
   Locations: CSd, VtNN (I).
5. Covers: sheaf of wheat design; spine: blindstamped filigree design, goldstamped 'MARGARET FULLER | OSSOLI' in ³/₁₆″ type.
   Locations: MAm, TxDN.
6. Covers: sheaf of wheat design; spine: blindstamped filigree design, goldstamped 'MARGARET FULLER | OSSOLI' in ¹/₈″ type.
   Location: InU (II).

Note: Copies with advertisements for Phillips, Sampson publications have been noted:

1. [I, 353–360]: MAm.
2. [II, 353–356]: FTaSU, FU, InU (II), MsU, TxDN.

A 7.1.f
Sixth printing: Boston: Phillips, Sampson and Company, 1857.

I: [1]⁴ 2–8⁶ 9² 9*⁴ 10–16⁶ 17² 17*⁴ 18–29⁶ 30²

II: [a]² 1–29⁶ 30²

Binding: Black S cloth (fine-ribbed). Front and back covers: sheaf of wheat design inside border at each corner. Spine: blindstamped filigree design with 'MARGARET FULLER | OSSOLI' in ³/₁₆″ type.

Location: MiMarqN.

Note: A copy of vol. II with advertisements on pp. [353]–[358] has been noted: MiMarqN.

A 7.1.g
Seventh printing: Boston: Brown, Taggard and Chase; New York: Sheldon & Co.; Philadelphia: J. B. Lippincott & Co.; London: Sampson Low, Son & Co., 1860.

I: [1]–32⁶ 33⁴

II: [a]¹ 1–29⁶ 30²

Contents: Same as in the first printing, except: *I:* tipped-in frontispiece facing title page: Plumbe daguerreotype; pp. 3–6: 'PREFACE' signed 'ARTHUR B. FULLER'; pp. 7–8: contents for vol. I; p. 353: 'APPENDIX.'; p. 354: blank; pp. 355–372: 'A. Thomas Fuller and His Descendants.'; pp. 373–386: 'B. Memorial of Mrs. Margaret Fuller, By Her Son, Richard F. Fuller.'; pp. 387–390: 'C.', poems "The Ascended Saint," "Eugene Fuller," "Margaret Fuller Ossoli," by Mrs. J. H. Hanaford.

Typography and paper: 7⁷/₈" × 4³/₄"; wove paper; 33 lines per page. Running heads: same as in the first printing, except: *I:* rectos: pp. 357–389: 'APPENDIX.'; versos: pp. 356–390: 'APPENDIX.'.

Binding: Black S cloth (fine-ribbed). Front and back covers: blindstamped triple-ruled border with 3³/₄" ornament in center. Spine: blindstamped bands and single filigree design with goldstamped 'MARGARET | FULLER'S | WORKS | [rule] | MEM-OIR | [rule] | VOL. I. [II.] | BROWN, TAGGARD & CHASE'. Flyleaves. Yellow endpapers. All edges trimmed.

Locations: MA, NHi.

Publication: Announced as to be published "soon" in *Bookseller's Medium and Publisher's Circular,* 15 October 1859, p. 98. Advertised as "Ready in a Few Days," *Bookseller's Medium and Publisher's Circular,* 16 January 1860, p. 218, and 1 February 1860, p. 244. Advertised as "Ready in a Few Days" in *Boston Daily Evening Transcript,* 9 January 1860, p. 3, and *Boston Daily Advertiser,* 11 January 1860, p. 2.

Note: Vol. I, leaf 33₄ is canceled.

A 7.1.h
Eighth printing: Boston: Brown, Taggard and Chase; New York: Sheldon & Co.; Philadelphia: J. B. Lippincott & Co.; London: Sampson Low, Son & Co., 1862.

Binding: Same as in the seventh printing, except: spine: goldstamped 'BROWN TAGGARD' at bottom.

Location: MNatM.

A 7.1.i
Ninth printing: New York: The Tribune Association, 1869.

I: [1–16¹² 17⁴]

II: [1² 2–15¹² 16⁸]

Contents: Same as in the seventh printing, except that the frontispiece is an engraving of Fuller's head and shoulders derived from a painting by Chappel (the entire Chappel painting is the frontispiece in Madeleine B. Stern, *The Life of Margaret Fuller* [New York: E. P. Dutton, 1942]).

Binding: L cloth (morocco); color variations listed below. Front and back covers: blindstamped single-ruled border with 2⁷/₈" ornament in center. Spine: goldstamped '[ornamental band] | MEMOIRS | OF | MARGARET | FULLER | OSSOLI. | VOL I [II] | TRIBUNE | [ornamental band]'. Flyleaves. Green endpapers. All edges trimmed.

1. Dark brown cloth.
   Locations: OCIW, PHC.

2. Dark reddish orange cloth.
   Location: WM.
3. Green cloth.
   Location: MH.
4. Medium purple cloth.
   Locations: CaBVaU, InU, JM, KMK (I), VtSjA, VtWinoS (I).

Publication: Price: six-volume Tribune edition of Fuller's works, $10.00 per set. Inscribed copy: WM (presentation copy from Horace Greeley, 1869).

A 7.1.j
Tenth printing: Boston: Roberts Brothers, 1874.

I: [1–16¹² 17⁴]

II: [1–14¹² 15¹⁰]

Contents: Same as in the seventh printing (with the Plumbe daguerreotype serving as the frontispiece).

Binding: L cloth (morocco); color variations listed below. Front and back covers: blindstamped double band with perpendicular lines. Spine: blindstamped bands with goldstamped 'MARGARET | FULLER'S | WORKS | [ornamental rule] | MEMOIRS. | [rule] | VOL. I. [II.] | [ornamental rule] | R [star-like publisher's device] B'. Flyleaves. Brown endpapers. All edges trimmed.

1. Dark green cloth.
   Locations: IP, MWC, MdBP, OO.
2. Dark reddish brown cloth.
   Location: BL.
3. Dark reddish orange cloth.
   Locations: InIB, JM, LNHT, MeBa, OCU, VtU, WMU, WU.
4. Dark reddish purple cloth.
   Locations: MWA, ViU.

Publication: According to the Roberts Brothers' cost books, 280 copies were printed and bound as of 1 February 1874. Mrs. Arthur B. Fuller retained the plates and received 10 percent on the retail price of each copy sold. Price: $3.00 per set. Inscribed copies: MCo [rebound] (presentation copy from Roberts Brothers, July 1874), ViU (January 1875).

Note: A set with advertisements at [I, 391–396] and [II, 353–358] for Robert Brothers publications has been noted: IP.

SUBSEQUENT PRINTINGS

A 7.1.k
Eleventh printing: Boston: Roberts Brothers, 1875.

According to the Roberts Brothers' cost books, 280 copies were printed between 24 February and 14 April 1875. Price: $3.00 per set.

A 7.1.l
Twelfth printing: Boston: Roberts Brothers, 1881.

Inscribed copy: NNC (25 December 1882).

A 7.1.m
Thirteenth printing: Boston: Roberts Brothers, 1884.

According to the Roberts Brothers' cost books, at least 310 copies were printed by 7 April 1884 and sold by July 1886. Price: $3.00 per set. Also noted: a second issue, bound as two volumes in one; a third issue, with the sheets of this printing (with Roberts Brothers title pages) bound in two volumes in Little, Brown and Company casings; and a fourth issue, with the sheets of this printing (with Roberts Brothers title pages) bound as two volumes in one in Little, Brown and Company casings.

A 7.1.n
Fourteenth printing: New York: Burt Franklin Publishers, 1973.

Facsimile of the 1884 text, bound in one volume. 350 copies printed. Published September 1973.

ENGLISH EDITIONS

A 7.1E
First English edition, only printing (1852)

MEMOIRS

OF

MARGARET FULLER OSSOLI.

IN THREE VOLUMES.
VOL. I.

"Only a learned and a manly soul
   I purposed her, that should with even powers
The rock, the spindle, and the shears control
   Of destiny, and spin her own free hours."
                                    BEN JONSON.

"Però che ogni diletto nostro è doglia
Sta in sì e nò saper, voler, potere;
Adunque quel sol può, che col dovere
Ne trae la ragion fuor di sua soglia.

Adunque tu' lettor di queste note,
S'a te vuoi esser buono, e agli altri caro,
Vogli sempre poter quel che tu debbi."
                                    LEONARDO DA VINCI.

LONDON:
RICHARD BENTLEY, NEW BURLINGTON STREET,
Publisher in Ordinary to Her Majesty.
1852.

A 7.1E: 7¹³⁄₁₆″ × 4⁷⁄₈″

I: [i–iii] iv [1–3] 4–70 [71–73] 74–186 [187–189] 190–264 [265–267] 268–314

II: [i–iii] iv [1] 2–118 [119–121] 122–168 [169–171] 172–325 [326]

III: [i–iii] iv [1–3] 4–73 [74–77] 78–306 [307–309] 310–336

I: [A]² B–I¹² K–O¹² P²

II: [A]² B–I¹² K–O¹² P⁸

III: [A]² B–I¹² K–P¹²

Contents: I: p. i: title page; p. ii: 'LONDON: | B. CLAY, PRINTER, BREAD STREET HILL.'; pp. iii–iv: contents for vol. I; p. 1: same as I.9 in American edition; p. 2: same as I.10 in American edition; pp. 3–70: 'I. Youth.'; p. 71: same as I.59 in American edition; p. 72: same as I.60 in American edition; pp. 73–186: 'II. Cambridge.'; p. 187: same as I.143 in American edition; p. 188: same as I.144 in American edition; pp. 189–264: 'III. Groton and Providence.'; p. 265: same as I.199 in American edition; p. 266: same as I.200 in American edition; pp. 267–314: 'IV. Visits to Concord.'.

II: p. i: title page; p. ii: printer's page (same as I.ii); pp. iii–iv: contents for vol. II; pp. 1–118: 'IV. Visits to Concord, (Continued.)'; p. 119: same as I.317 in American edition; p. 120: blank; pp. 121–168: 'V. Conversations in Boston.'; p. 169: same as II.3 in American edition; p. 170: same as II.4 in American edition; pp. 171–325: 'VI. Jamaica Plain.'; p. 326: blank.

III: p. i: title page; p. ii: printer's page (same as I.ii); pp. iii–iv: contents for vol. III; p. 1: same as II.117 in American edition; p. 2: same as II.118 in American edition; pp. 3–73: 'VII. New York.'; p. 74: blank; p. 75: same as II.169 in American edition; p. 76: same as II.170 in American edition; pp. 77–306: 'VIII. Europe.'; p. 307: same as II.331 in American edition; p. 308: same as II.332 in American edition; pp. 309–336: 'IX. Homeward.'.

Typography and paper: 7¹³/₁₆″ × 4⁷/₈″; wove paper; 25 lines per page. Running heads: similar to those in the American edition.

Binding: S cloth (fine-ribbed); color variations listed below. Front and back covers: blindstamped triple-ruled border with filigree designs at corners between inner rules and 4¹/₂″ ornament in center. Spine: blindstamped ornament in middle with gold-stamped 'MEMOIRS | OF | MARGARET | FULLER | OSSOLI | [rule] | VOL. I. [II.] [III.] | LONDON | BENTLEY.'. Light yellow endpapers. All edges untrimmed and uncut.

1. Brown cloth.
   Locations: BLdU, BO.
2. Yellow white cloth.
   Locations: CtY, JM, ViU.

Publication: Advertised as "Will Publish" in January in *Athenæum,* no. 1263 (10 January 1852), 38, and *Literary Gazette,* 36 (10 January 1852), 48. Listed under "New Publications" in *Athenæum,* no. 1266 (31 January 1852), 134. Price: 31s. 6 p. per set. Inscribed copy: BL (deposit copy, 9 February 1852).

Note one: The following are canceled leafs: vol. I, leaf P₂; vol. II, leaf P₈.

Note two: A copy of the first, second, or third printing of the American edition served as the basis for the first English edition, which has the "written in 1839" reading corresponding to I.98.20 (see A 7.1.d).

A 7.2E
Second English edition, only printing (1861)

SUMMER ON THE LAKES. | WITH AUTOBIOGRAPHY. | BY | MARGARET FULLER
OSSOLI. | And Memoir, | BY | RALPH WALDO EMERSON, W. H. CHANNING, | AND
OTHERS. | LONDON: | WARD AND LOCK, FLEET STREET. | MDCCCLXI.

The text of *Memoirs* through 1840 is on pp. [249]–360. For full information, see A 4.1E,
first English edition, only printing, of *Summer on the Lakes*.

GERMAN EDITION

A 7.1G
First German edition, only printing (1866)

Margaret Fuller-Ossoli. Ein amerikanisches Frauenbild [consisting of an autobiography, with notices of her life by R. W. Emerson, W. H. Channing, *etc.* Trans. and ed.]
von E. Castell. Berlin, 1866.

Note: This information was taken from *British Museum Catalogue of Printed Books*,
80, 520; no copies have been located for inspection.

A 8 WOMAN IN THE NINETEENTH CENTURY, AND KINDRED PAPERS

A 8.1.a
Only edition, first printing (1855)

WOMAN

IN THE

NINETEENTH CENTURY,

AND

KINDRED PAPERS

RELATING TO THE

Sphere, Condition and Duties, of Woman.

BY

MARGARET FULLER OSSOLI.

EDITED BY HER BROTHER,
ARTHUR B. FULLER.

WITH AN INTRODUCTION BY HORACE GREELEY.

———◆———

BOSTON:
PUBLISHED BY JOHN P. JEWETT & COMPANY.
CLEVELAND, OHIO:
JEWETT, PROCTOR & WORTHINGTON.
NEW YORK: SHELDON, LAMPORT & CO.
1855.

A 8.1.a: 7⅝" × 4¾"

[i–iii] iv–viii [ix] x [xi] xii [xiii] xiv [15] 16–179 [180–183] 184–216 [217] 218–227 [228] 229–230 [231] 232–236 [237] 238–240 [241] 242–249 [250] 251–255 [256] 257–260 [261] 262–265 [266] 267–268 [269] 270–275 [276] 277–279 [280] 281–285 [286] 287 [288] 289–294 [295] 296–297 [298] 299 [300] 301–309 [310] 311–313 [314] 315–319 [320] 321–324 [325] 326–334 [335] 336–337 [338–341] 342–393 [394–397] 398–428

[1]–35^6 36^4

Contents: Tipped-in frontispiece facing title page: Plumbe daguerreotype; p. i: title page; p. ii: 'Entered according to Act of Congress, in the year 1855, by | A. B. FULLER, | In the Clerk's Office of the District Court of the District of Massachusetts. | Stereotyped by | HOBART & ROBBINS, | New England Type and Stereotype Foundry, | BOSTON.'; pp. iii–viii: 'PREFACE' signed 'A.B.F. | BOSTON, *May* 10*th*, 1855.'; pp. ix–x: 'INTRODUCTION' signed 'H. GREELEY.'; pp. xi–xii: contents; pp. xiii–xiv: 'PREFACE' to *Woman in the Nineteenth Century;* pp. 15–179: text of *Woman in the Nineteenth Century;* p. 180: blank; p. 181: 'PART II. | [rule] | MISCELLANIES.'; p. 182: blank; pp. 183–216: 'Aglauron and Laurie'; pp. 217–227: 'The Wrongs of American Women. The Duty of American Women.'; pp. 228–230: 'George Sand'; pp. 231–236: 'From a Notice of George Sand'; pp. 237–240: 'From a Criticism on "Consuelo" '; pp. 241–249: 'Jenny Lind, the "Consuelo" of George Sand'; pp. 250–255: 'Caroline'; pp. 256–260: 'Ever-Growing Lives'; pp. 261–265: 'Household Nobleness'; pp. 266–268: ' "Glumdalclitches" '; pp. 269–275: ' "Ellen; or, Forgive and Forget" '; pp. 276–279: ' "Courrier des Etats Unis" '; pp. 280–285: ' "Courrier des Etats Unis." Our Protégée, Queen Victoria.'; pp. 286–287: 'On Books of Travel'; pp. 288–294: 'Review of "Memoirs and Essays, by Mrs. Jameson" '; pp. 295–297: 'Woman's Influence Over the Insane'; pp. 298–299: 'From a Criticism on Browning's Poems'; pp. 300–309: 'Christmas'; pp. 310–313: 'Children's Books'; pp. 314–319: 'Woman in Poverty'; pp. 320–324: 'The Irish Character'; pp. 325–334: 'The Irish Character'; pp. 335–337: 'Educate Men and Women as Souls'; p. 338: blank; p. 339: 'PART III. | [rule] | EXTRACTS FROM JOURNALS AND LETTERS.'; p. 340: blank; pp. 341–393: 'Extracts from Journals and Letters'; p. 394: blank; p. 395: 'APPENDIX.'; p. 396: blank; pp. 397–428: appendix.

Typography and paper: 7^5/$_8$" × 4^3/$_4$"; wove paper; 30 lines per page. Running heads: rectos: pp. v–vii: 'PREFACE.'; pp. 17–37: 'NINETEENTH CENTURY.'; pp. 39–179: similar to those in the 1845 edition (see A 5.1.a^1); pp. 185–337: titles of selections; p. 343: 'EXTRACT FROM JOURNAL.'; p. 345: 'LETTER TO M.'; pp. 347–349: 'TO HER BROTHER.'; p. 351: 'TO A YOUNG FRIEND.'; pp. 353–355: 'LINES.'; pp. 357–359: 'TO A YOUNG FRIEND.'; pp. 361–363: 'TO THE SAME.'; p. 365: 'TO HER BROTHER, R.'; pp. 367–371: 'TO MISS R.'; p. 373: 'TO HER BROTHER, R.'; p. 375: 'TO MAZZINI.'; p. 377: 'TO MR. AND MRS. SPRING.'; p. 379: 'TO HER BROTHER, R.'; pp. 381–383: 'TO MR. AND MRS. S.'; pp. 385–387: 'TO ———.'; pp. 389–393: 'LETTER FROM HON. LEWIS CASS, JR.'; pp. 399–427: 'APPENDIX.'; versos: pp. iv–viii: 'PREFACE.'; p. x: 'INTRODUCTION.'; p. xii: 'CONTENTS.'; p. xiv: 'PREFACE.'; pp. 16–36: 'WOMAN IN THE'; pp. 38–178: 'WOMAN IN THE NINETEENTH CENTURY.'; pp. 184–336, 342–392: 'MISCELLANIES.'; pp. 398–428: 'APPENDIX.'.

Binding: S cloth (fine-ribbed); color variations listed below. Front and back covers: blindstamped double-ruled border with design in each corner and 2^{13}/$_{16}$" ornamental circle containing the publisher's initials in center. Spine: blindstamped rules and ornaments with goldstamped 'WOMAN | IN THE | NINETEENTH CENTURY | JEWETT & CO.' Flyleaves. Pale yellow endpapers. All edges trimmed.

1. Black cloth.
    Locations: CaOWtU, MAm, NFQC, ODW, OHi, PPT, PU, TxLT, ViU, VtMiM.

2. Brown cloth.
   Locations: CaOLU, ICarbS, JM, MBC, MC, MNBedf, NHi, NSbSU, OCIW, PBm, PP, PU, RPA.
3. Dark brown cloth.
   Locations: BL, CSmH, CU-S, DGU, JM, LNHT, MHarF, MWA, MWay, MiU, NAIU, OU, PP, TM, TxDW, ViNO.
4. Light brown cloth.
   Locations: JM, MMe, MiBsA, MnHi.

Publication: Listed as published since 15 May in *Norton's Literary Gazette,* n.s. 2 (1 June 1855), 241. Price: $1.00. Inscribed copies: CU-S (presentation copy from Arthur B. Fuller, May 1855), MWA (23 May 1855), MBC (7 June 1855).

Note one: An English importation by Trübner listed as "Just Received from America," *Athenæum,* no. 1444 (30 June 1855), 772, and by Sampson Low as "New Importation—This Day" in *Publishers' Circular and Booksellers' Record,* 18 (2 July 1855), 249. Price: 6s. Neither apparently is a separate issue; no copies in a Trübner or a Sampson Low binding, or with a cancel title page, have been reported.

Note two: Horace Greeley wrote Arthur B. Fuller on 1 March 1855 that he had "carefully revised" the text of *Woman in the Nineteenth Century* (see A 5.1.a), "making some very slight verbal alterations" to "express the author's thought more clearly" (MH).

A 8.1.b
Second printing: Boston: John P. Jewett & Company; Cleveland, Ohio: Jewett, Proctor & Worthington; New York: Sheldon, Lamport & Co., 1855.

Title page states that this is the 'THIRD THOUSAND'.

Binding: S cloth (fine-ribbed); color variations listed below. Cover and spine stamping same as in the first printing.

1. Black cloth.
   Locations: BMR, JM, NhHi, TMU.
2. Brown cloth.
   Locations: ArU, DLC, MMeT, MeB, OYesA.
3. Dark brown cloth.
   Locations: CoFS, MeB, TxDaM.
4. Light brown cloth.
   Locations: JM, NBiSu, RNR, ViHarT.

Publication: Inscribed copy: MH [rebound] (13 June 1855).

A 8.1.c
Third printing: Boston: John P. Jewett & Company; Cleveland, Ohio: Jewett, Proctor & Worthington; New York: Sheldon, Lamport & Co., 1857.

Title page states that this is the 'THIRD THOUSAND'.

Binding: S cloth (fine-ribbed); color variations listed below. Cover and spine stamping same as in the first printing.

1. Black cloth.
   Location: JM.
2. Dark brown cloth.
   Location: OCIWHi.

Publication: Inscribed copy: JM (1857).

A 8.1.d
Fourth printing: Boston: Brown, Taggard and Chase; New York: Sheldon & Co.; Philadelphia: J. B. Lippincott & Co.; London: Sampson Low, Son & Co., 1860.

[1–17^{12} 18^{6}]

Contents: pp. i–297: same as in the first printing; pp. 298–299: 'The Deaf and Dumb'; pp. 300–394: same as in the first printing; p. 395: 'PART IV. | [rule] | MEMORIALS OF MARGARET FULLER OSSOLI.'; p. 396: blank; pp. 397–420: 'Memorials of Margaret Fuller Ossoli' by Horace Greeley, Mrs. A. A. Livermore, and Mrs. J. H. Hanaford.

Typography and paper: Same as in the first printing, except: running heads: rectos: pp. 399–419: 'MARGARET FULLER OSSOLI.'; versos: pp. 398–418: 'MEMORIALS OF'; p. 420: 'MEMORIALS OF MARGARET FULLER OSSOLI.'.

Binding: Black S cloth (fine-ribbed). Front and back covers: blindstamped triple-ruled border with 3³/₄″ ornament in center. Spine: blindstamped bands and single filigree design with goldstamped 'MARGARET | FULLER'S | WORKS | [rule] | WOMAN | IN THE | NINETEENTH | CENTURY, &C. | BROWN, TAGGARD & CHASE'. Flyleaves. Yellow endpapers. All edges trimmed.

Locations: CCC, IEN.

Publication: Announced as to be published "soon" in *Bookseller's Medium and Publisher's Circular,* 15 October 1859, p. 98. Advertised as "Ready in a Few Days" in *Bookseller's Medium and Publisher's Circular,* 16 January 1860, p. 218, and 1 February 1860, p. 244; *Boston Daily Evening Transcript,* 9 January 1860, p. 3; and *Boston Daily Advertiser,* 11 January 1860, p. 2. Inscribed copy: CaOTY [rebound] (5 September 1860).

A 8.1.e
Fifth printing: Boston: Brown, Taggard and Chase; New York: Sheldon & Co.; Philadelphia: J. B. Lippincott & Co.; London: Sampson Low, Son & Co., 1862.

Contents: Same as in the fourth printing.

Location: JM.

Note one: The one located copy has been rebound in library cloth; collation and binding information are unavailable.

A 8.1.f
Sixth printing: New York: The Tribune Association, 1869.

[1–17^{12} 18^{6}]

Contents: pp. i–297: same as in the fourth printing; pp. 298–310: 'Pochahontas'; pp. 311–314: 'Children's Books'; pp. 315–320: 'Woman in Poverty'; pp. 321–325: 'The Irish Character'; pp. 326–335: 'The Irish Character'; pp. 336–338: 'Educate Men and Women as Souls'; pp. 339–420: same as in the fourth printing.

Binding: L cloth (morocco); color variations listed below. Front and back covers: blindstamped single-ruled border with 2⁷/₈″ ornament in center. Spine: goldstamped '[ornamental band] | WOMAN | IN THE | NINETEENTH CENTURY, | AND | KINDRED PAPERS. | MARGARET | FULLER | OSSOLI. | TRIBUNE | [ornamental band]'. Flyleaves. Green endpapers. All edges trimmed.

1. Dark brown cloth.
   Location: TNJ-P.

2. Dark reddish orange cloth.
   Locations: InIB, JM, MAt.
3. Green cloth.
   Locations: NN, NjNbS.
4. Medium purple cloth.
   Locations: MB, VtSjA.

Publication: Price: six-volume Tribune edition of Fuller's works, $10.00 per set. Inscribed copy: TNJ-P (19 November 1869).

A 8.1.g
Seventh printing: Boston: Roberts Brothers, 1874.

[1–17^{12} 18^6]

Contents: Same as in the sixth printing.

Binding: L cloth (morocco); color variations listed below. Front and back covers: blindstamped double band with perpendicular lines. Spine: blindstamped bands with goldstamped 'MARGARET | FULLER'S | WORKS | [ornamental rule] | WOMAN | IN THE | 19TH CENTURY. | [ornamental rule] | R [star-like publisher's device] B'. Flyleaves. Brown endpapers. All edges trimmed.

1. Dark green cloth.
   Locations: MWC, MdBP, NSsS.
2. Dark reddish brown cloth.
   Location: BL.
3. Dark reddish orange cloth.
   Locations: CaOHM, InIB, JM, MeBa, OCU.
4. Dark reddish purple cloth.
   Locations: MHi, MWA, NBu.

Publication: According to the Roberts Brothers' cost books, 280 copies were printed and bound as of 1 February 1874. Mrs. Arthur B. Fuller retained the plates and received 10 percent on the retail price of each copy sold. Price: $1.50. Inscribed copy: NBu (April 1874).

SUBSEQUENT PRINTINGS

A 8.1.h
Eighth printing: Boston: Roberts Brothers, 1875.

According to the Roberts Brothers' cost books, 392 copies were printed between 24 February and 14 April 1875. Price: $1.50.

A 8.1.i
Ninth printing: Boston: Roberts Brothers, 1884.

According to the Roberts Brothers' cost books, 280 copies were printed as of 22 October 1884. Price: $1.50.

A 8.1.j
Tenth printing: Boston: Roberts Brothers, 1893.

According to the Roberts Brothers' cost books, approximately 240 copies were printed as of 8 March 1893. A second issue, with the sheets of this printing (with the Roberts Brothers title page) bound in Little, Brown and Company casings, has been noted.

A 8.1.k
Eleventh printing: Westport, Conn.: Greenwood Press, 1968.

Facsimile of the 1874 text. 533 copies printed. Published 31 January 1969.

A 8.1.l
Twelfth printing: New York: Source Book Press, 1970.

Facsimile of the 1855 text.

A 8.1.m
Thirteenth printing: New York: W. W. Norton & Company, Inc., 1971.

Facsimile of the 1855 text of *Woman in the Nineteenth Century* and "Appendix" only. Stiff paper wrappers. 5,000 copies printed. Published November 1971.

A 8.1.n
Fourteenth printing: Freeport, N.Y.: Books for Libraries Press, 1972.

Facsimile of the 1855 text.

A 9 AT HOME AND ABROAD

A 9.1.a
Only edition, first printing (1856)

AT HOME AND ABROAD,

OR

THINGS AND THOUGHTS

IN

America and Europe.

BY

MARGARET FULLER OSSOLI,

AUTHOR OF "WOMAN IN THE NINETEENTH CENTURY," "PAPERS ON LITERATURE
AND ART," ETC.

EDITED BY HER BROTHER,

ARTHUR B. FULLER.

BOSTON:
CROSBY, NICHOLS, AND COMPANY.

LONDON:
SAMPSON LOW, SON, & CO.

1 8 5 6.

A 9.1.a: 7⁹/₁₆″ × 5″

Two issues have been noted.

A 9.1.a¹
First issue

[i–iii] iv–x [xi–xii] [1–3] 4–10 [11] 12–31 [32] 33–51 [52] 53–57 [58] 59–77 [78] 79–102 [103] 104–116 [117–119] 120–126 [127] 128–133 [134] 135–138 [139] 140–146 [147] 148–157 [158] 159–163 [164] 165–168 [169] 170–175 [176] 177–185 [186] 187–196 [197] 198–203 [204] 205–212 [213] 214–219 [220] 221–227 [228] 229–235 [236] 237–241 [242] 243–249 [250] 251–256 [257] 258–268 [269] 270–275 [276] 277–291 [292] 293–302 [303] 304–309 [310] 311–327 [328] 329–335 [336] 337–345 [346] 347–354 [355] 356–362 [363] 364–379 [380] 381–389 [390] 391–400 [401] 402–409 [410] 411–421 [422–425] 426–440 [441–443] 444–466 [467–468]

[a]⁶ 1–39⁶

Contents: p. i: title page; p. ii: 'Entered according to Act of Congress, in the year 1856, by | ARTHUR B. FULLER, | in the Clerk's Office of the District Court of the District of Massachusetts. | CAMBRIDGE: | STEREOTYPED AND PRINTED BY METCALF AND COMPANY.'; pp. iii–x: 'PREFACE.' signed 'A. B. F. | BOSTON, March 1, 1856.'; p. xi: contents; p. xii: blank; p. 1: 'PART I. | SUMMER ON THE LAKES.'; p. 2: poems, "Summer days of busy leisure . . ." and "Some dried grass-tufts from the wide flowery field . . ."; pp. 3–116: text of *Summer on the Lakes;* p. 117: 'PART II. | THINGS AND THOUGHTS IN EUROPE.'; p. 118: blank; pp. 119–421: texts of Fuller's travel letters to the *New-York Tribune;* p. 422: blank; p. 423: 'PART III. | LETTERS FROM ABROAD TO FRIENDS | AT HOME.'; p. 424: blank; pp. 425–440: texts of letters; p. 441: 'PART IV. | HOMEWARD VOYAGE, AND MEMORIALS.'; p. 442: blank; pp. 443–466: accounts of Fuller's voyage to America, the wreck of her ship at Fire Island, and memorials to her; p. 467: advertisement for other writings by Fuller offered for sale by Crosby, Nichols; p. 468: blank.

Typography and paper: 7⁹/₁₆″ × 5″; wove paper; 36 lines per page. Running heads: rectos: pp. v–ix: 'PREFACE.'; pp. 5–115: similar to those in the 1844 edition (see A 4.1.a¹); p. 121: 'MECHANICS' INSTITUTE.'; p. 123: 'PEACE AND WAR.'; p. 125: 'CHESTER.'; p. 129: 'REFORMERS.'; p. 131: 'WORDSWORTH.'; p. 133: 'MISS MARTINEAU.'; p. 135: 'KESWICK.'; p. 137: 'SCOTT AND BURNS.'; p. 141: 'BURNS.'; p. 143: 'THE BOOKSELLING TRADE.'; p. 145: 'CHALMERS.'; p. 149: 'PERTH.'; p. 151: 'LOCH KATRINE.'; p. 153: 'BEN LOMOND.'; p. 155: 'A NIGHT ON BEN LOMOND.'; p. 157: 'SCOTCH PEASANTRY.'; p. 159: 'GLASGOW.'; p. 161: 'STIRLING CASTLE.'; p. 163: 'SCOTT'S TOMB.'; p. 165: 'WARWICK CASTLE.'; p. 167: 'MARTINEAU AND FOX.'; p. 171: 'JOANNA BAILLIE.'; p. 173: 'THE PEOPLE'S JOURNAL.'; p. 175: 'THOM.'; p. 177: 'ZOÖLOGICAL GARDENS.'; p. 179: 'A GILPIN EXCURSION.'; p. 181: 'MAZZINI.'; pp. 183–185: 'CARLYLE.'; p. 187: 'WASHING ESTABLISHMENT.'; p. 189: 'RACHEL.'; p. 191: 'DUMAS.'; p. 193: 'THE SORBONNE.'; p. 195: 'LE MENNAIS AND BÉRANGER.'; p. 199: 'TURNER'S PICTURES.'; p. 201: 'THE OPERA.'; p. 203: 'THE LETHEON.'; p. 205: 'FOURIER.'; p. 207: 'THE CHAMBER OF DEPUTIES.'; p. 209: 'INTERNATIONAL EXCHANGE OF BOOKS.'; p. 211: 'SCHOOL FOR IDIOTS.'; p. 215: 'LYONS AND ITS WEAVERS.'; p. 217: 'CLIMATE OF ITALY.'; p. 219: 'PASSAGE FROM LEGHORN.'; p. 221: 'STUDIO OF MACDONALD.'; p. 223: 'ITALIAN PAINTERS.'; p. 225: 'PIUS IX. AND HIS MEASURES.'; p. 227: 'THE CONTEMPORANEO.'; p. 229: 'ASSISI.'; p. 231: 'FLORENCE.'; p. 233: 'VENICE.'; p. 235: 'ITALIAN AFFAIRS.'; p. 237: 'MILAN.'; p. 239: 'HATRED OF AUSTRIAN RULE.'; p. 241: 'PARMA.'; p. 243: 'LIBERTY OF THE PRESS.'; p. 245: 'FÊTE AT FLORENCE.'; p. 247: 'DOCILITY OF THE PEOPLE.'; p. 249: 'SYMPATHY FROM AMERICA.'; p. 251: 'AMERICANS IN EUROPE.'; p. 253: 'PRESENT STATE OF EUROPE.'; p. 255: 'THE ABOLITIONISTS.'; p. 259: 'ROME IN ITS VARIOUS ASPECTS.';

p. 261: 'CEMETERY OF SANTO SPIRITO.'; p. 263: 'THE POPE.'; p. 265: 'INAUGURA-
TION OF THE COUNCIL.'; p. 267: 'THE SALTERELLO.'; p. 271: 'TAKING THE VEIL.'; p.
273: 'EXCITEMENT AT NAPLES.'; p. 275: 'PARMA.'; p. 277: 'A POOR YOUTH IN
ROME.'; p. 279: 'THE JESUITS.'; p. 281: 'CONSUL FOR THE UNITED STATES.'; p. 283:
'SPEECH TO THE CONSISTORY.'; pp. 285–289: 'LETTER OF MAZZINI.'; p. 291:
'AMERICAN ADDRESS TO THE POPE.'; p. 293: 'FUNERAL OF DON CARLO TORLO-
NIA.'; p. 295: 'EXCITEMENTS THROUGHOUT ITALY.'; p. 297: 'THE BAMBINO.'; p. 299:
'EXHIBITION BY THE PROPAGANDA.'; p. 301: 'NEWS FROM NAPLES, FRANCE, AND
SPAIN.'; p. 305: 'DETHRONEMENT OF LOUIS PHILIPPE.'; p. 307: 'OBLATIONS TO
THE CAUSE OF LIBERTY.'; p. 309: 'FREEDOM FOR ITALY.'; p. 311: 'MILANESE AD-
DRESS TO THE GERMANS.'; pp. 313–315: 'ADDRESS TO NATIONS UNDER AUS-
TRIAN RULE.'; p. 317: 'MICKIEWICZ IN FLORENCE.'; p. 319: 'SPEECH OF MICKIEW-
ICZ.'; p. 321: 'WEAKNESS OF PIUS IX.'; p. 323: 'DISAPPOINTMENT OF THE PEOPLE.';
p. 325: 'RESULTS OF THE POPE'S DEFECTION.'; p. 327: 'THE TRUE AMERICA.'; p.
329: 'REVIEW OF THE COURSE OF PIUS IX.'; p. 331: 'NOBLENESS VERSUS SELFISH-
NESS.'; p. 333: 'CHARLES ALBERT.'; p. 335: 'SUMMER AMONG THE MOUNTAINS.';
p. 337: 'AFFAIRS AT ROME.'; p. 339: 'SAINT CECILIA.'; p. 341: 'DEMONSTRATION ON
THE QUIRINAL.'; p. 343: 'THE POPE'S FLIGHT.'; p. 345: 'DON TIRLONE.'; p. 347: 'FAIR
OF ST. EUSTACHIO.'; p. 349: 'MORAL ASPECT OF ITALIAN REVOLUTION.'; pp. 351–
353: 'THE POPE'S MANIFESTO.'; p. 357: 'OPENING OF THE ASSEMBLY.'; p. 359:
'INAUGURATION OF THE REPUBLIC.'; p. 361: 'SYMPATHY HOPED FROM AMERICA.';
p. 365: 'MAZZINI.'; p. 367: 'ADDRESS OF MAZZINI.'; p. 369: 'AMERICAN ARTISTS.'; p.
371: 'SCULPTORS.'; p. 373: 'CRAWFORD'S WASHINGTON.'; p. 375: 'MISTAKEN
DEALINGS WITH ARTISTS.'; p. 377: 'TRIALS OF AN ARTIST.'; p. 379: 'AN AVE
MARIA.'; p. 381: 'ITALY PROTESTANT.'; p. 383: 'EFFECTS OF WAR.'; p. 385: 'PRINC-
ESS BELGIOIOSO.'; p. 387: 'APPEAL TO AMERICA.'; p. 389: 'POSSIBLE FUTURE OF
ROME.'; pp. 391–395: 'LETTER OF THE TRIUMVIRS.'; p. 397: 'ATTACK ON THE CITY.';
p. 399: 'HAVOC OF THE SIEGE.'; p. 403: 'ANSWERS TO OUDINOT.'; p. 405: 'INFA-
MOUS CONDUCT OF FRANCE.'; p. 407: 'NOBLE MEN SACRIFICED.'; p. 409: 'THE
CRISIS APPROACHING.'; p. 411: 'THE FRENCH ENTER ROME.'; p. 413: 'DEPARTURE
OF GARIBALDI.'; p. 415: 'MARTIAL LAW DECLARED.'; p. 417: 'CONDUCT OF MR.
CASS.'; p. 419: 'ADDRESS BY A ROMAN.'; p. 421: 'DUTY OF AMERICA.'; pp. 427–429:
'TO HER MOTHER.'; pp. 431–433: 'TO HER BROTHER.'; p. 435: 'TO R. W. EMERSON.';
p. 437: 'TO W. H. CHANNING.'; p. 439: 'TO HER MOTHER.'; pp. 445–447: 'LETTER OF
BAYARD TAYLOR.'; p. 449: 'MRS. HASTY'S NARRATIVE.'; p. 451: 'PASSENGERS
LOST IN THE ELIZABETH.'; pp. 453–455: 'BIOGRAPHY OF MADAME OSSOLI.'; p.
457: 'C. P. CRANCH.'; p. 459: 'MARY C. AMES.'; p. 461: 'SLEEP SWEETLY, GENTLE
CHILD.'; p. 463: 'G. P. R. JAMES.'; p. 465: 'MONUMENT.'; versos: pp. iv–x: 'PRE-
FACE.'; pp. 4–116: 'SUMMER ON THE LAKES.'; pp. 120–420: 'THINGS AND
THOUGHTS IN EUROPE.'; pp. 426–440: 'LETTERS TO FRIENDS AT HOME.'; pp. 444–
454: 'HOMEWARD VOYAGE.'; pp. 456–466: 'MEMORIALS.'.

Binding: S cloth (fine-ribbed); color variations listed below. Front and back covers:
blindstamped border (variations listed below) with 3½" ornament containing publisher's initials in center. Spine: blindstamped crescent designs with goldstamped 'AT
HOME | AND | ABROAD | [rule] | MADAME OSSOLI | CROSBY, NICHOLS & CO'.
Flyleaves. Pale yellow endpapers. All edges trimmed.

1. Black cloth; triple-ruled border.
   Locations: BMR, CtU, JM, MBU, MWA, NRU, NcD, ODW, ViU.
2. Blue cloth; triple-ruled border.
   Locations: NBuU, RU, ScGF.
3. Brown cloth; triple-ruled border.
   Locations: CaOWtU, JM, MHi, MSa, MdBP, NGenoU, WvHM.

4. Dark brown cloth; triple-ruled border.
   Locations: CU-D, FU, GEU, InLP, MdBJ, MH, MHarF, NAIU, NBu, NIC, OrU, RHi.
5. Dark gray green cloth; triple-ruled border.
   Locations: CCC, JM, MiU, MnHi, OCIWHi, OHi.
6. Reddish purple cloth; triple-ruled border.
   Locations: CoU, IEN, JM, MMeT, MdU, MoKiT, NcWsW, NhHi, OC, OKentU, OMC, PPT, TxU.
7. Black cloth; scallop-rule border.
   Location: JM.

Publication: Listed as "in press" in *Criterion,* 1 (15 December 1855), 105. Advertised as "will be ready" on 27 March in *Boston Evening Transcript,* 25 March 1856, p. 3. Reviewed in *Boston Daily Evening Transcript,* 25 March 1856, p. 1. Listed in *American Publishers' Circular and Literary Gazette,* 1 (29 March 1856), 196, and in "New Publications," *Criterion,* 1 (29 March 1856), 350. Price: $1.25. Inscribed copies: NIC (23 March 1856), MH (18 April 1856).

A 9.1.a²
Second issue: London: Sampson Low, Son & Co., 1856.

American sheets (with first-issue title page) in English casings of deep green cloth. Front and back covers: blindstamped leaf and strapwork design. Spine: goldstamped '[leaf design] | AT HOME | AND | ABROAD | [rule] | OSSOLI | [leaf design] | SAMPSON LOW, | SON & CO.' at bottom.

Locations: BEU, CStbS.

Publication: Announced as ready "Shortly" in *Athenæum,* no. 1483 (29 March 1856), 383. Listed with "New Books" in *Athenæum,* no. 1485 (12 April 1856), 460. Price: 7s. 6d.

Note one: One copy noted with eight-page catalogue of Sampson Low publications, dated "January 1856," bound at end: CStbS.

A 9.1.b
Second printing: Boston: Crosby, Nichols, and Company; London: Sampson Low, Son & Co., 1856.

[1–20¹²]

Binding: S cloth (fine-ribbed); color variations listed below. Cover and spine stamping same as in the first printing.

1. Black cloth.
   Locations: NBC, NFQC.
2. Dark brown cloth.
   Locations: In, InNd.
3. Very purple blue cloth.
   Location: NBuHi.

A 9.1.c
Third printing: Boston: Crosby, Nichols, and Company; London: Sampson Low, Son & Co., 1856.

Title page states that this is the 'SECOND EDITION'.

[a]⁶ 1–39⁶

Binding: S cloth (fine-ribbed); color variations listed below. Cover and spine stamping same as in the first printing.

1. Brown cloth.
   Location: PMA.
2. Dark brown cloth.
   Locations: IDeKN, KPT, MWA, NjP, TxDN.
3. Reddish purple cloth.
   Locations: CaOLU, IDeKN, OKentU.
4. Very purple blue cloth.
   Locations: ArU, DLC.

Publication: Inscribed copies: NjP (5 June 1856), ArU (15 June 1856).

A 9.1.d
Fourth printing: Boston: Crosby, Nichols, and Company; London: Sampson Low, Son & Co., 1856.

Title page states that this is the 'SECOND EDITION'.

[1–20^{12}]

Binding: S cloth (fine-ribbed); color variations listed below. Cover and spine stamping same as in the first printing.

1. Black cloth.
   Locations: NBC, WaU.
2. Brown cloth.
   Locations: JM, MDee, MeB, NRU, ScU, WaTC.
3. Dark brown cloth.
   Locations: CaSSU, CtW, MWH, WU.
4. Red cloth.
   Locations: ArL, OU.
5. Reddish purple cloth.
   Location: TxU.

Publication: Inscribed copies: WU (28 May 1856), MWH (presentation copy from Richard F. Fuller, 29 October 1856).

A 9.1.e
Fifth printing: Boston: Crosby, Nichols, and Company; London: Sampson Low, Son & Co., 1856.

Title page states that this is the 'THIRD EDITION'.

[a]^6 1–39^6

Binding: S cloth (fine-ribbed); color variations listed below. Cover and spine stamping same as in the first printing.

1. Black cloth.
   Location: JM.
2. Brown cloth.
   Locations: ICM, JM, NGenoU.
3. Dark brown cloth.
   Locations: MWiW, NcU.
4. Dark gray green cloth.
   Location: MoKU.

5. Reddish purple cloth.
   Locations: MMar, MeWC.
6. Very purple blue cloth.
   Location: JM.

Publication: Inscribed copy: MeWC (5 June 1856).

A 9.1.f
Sixth printing: Boston: Crosby, Nichols, and Company; London: Sampson Low, Son &
Co., 1856.

Title page states that this is the 'THIRD EDITION'.

[1–20¹²]

Binding: Dark brown TR cloth (wavy-grained). Cover and spine stamping same as in
the first printing.

Location: AzU.

A 9.1.g
Seventh printing: Boston: Brown, Taggard and Chase; New York: Sheldon & Co.;
Philadelphia: J. B. Lippincott & Co.; London: Sampson Low, Son & Co., 1860.

[a]⁶ 1–39⁶

Contents: Same as in the first printing, except: p. 467: blank.

Binding: Black S cloth (fine-ribbed). Front and back covers: blindstamped triple-
ruled border with 3³/₄″ ornament in center. Spine: blindstamped bands and single
filigree design with goldstamped 'MARGARET | FULLER'S | WORKS | [rule] | HOME
| AND | ABROAD | BROWN, TAGGARD & CHASE'. Flyleaves. Yellow endpapers. All
edges trimmed.

Locations: KPT, MA.

Publication: Announced as to be published "soon" in *Bookseller's Medium and Publisher's Circular,* 15 October 1859, p. 98. Advertised as "Ready in a Few Days" in
Bookseller's Medium and Publisher's Circular, 16 January 1860, p. 218, and 1 February 1860, p. 244. Advertised as "Ready in a Few Days" in *Boston Daily Evening
Transcript,* 9 January 1860, p. 3, and *Boston Daily Avertiser,* 11 January 1860, p. 2.

A 9.1.h
Eighth printing: Boston: Brown, Taggard and Chase; New York: Sheldon & Co.; Philadelphia: J. B. Lippincott & Co.; London: Sampson Low, Son & Co., 1862.

Title page states that this is the 'NEW AND COMPLETE EDITION'.

[a]⁶ 1–39⁶

Contents: Same as in the first printing (including Crosby, Nichols advertisement on
p. 467).

Binding: Red S cloth (fine-ribbed). Cover stamping same as in the seventh printing.
Spine: goldstamped 'AT HOME | AND | ABROAD | [rule] | MARGARET FULLER'.

Location: FTaSU.

A 9.1.i
Ninth printing: New York: The Tribune Association, 1869.

Title page states that this is the 'NEW AND COMPLETE EDITION'.

[1^2 2–20^{12} 21^6]

Contents: Same as in the first printing (including Crosby, Nichols advertisement on p. 467).

Binding: L cloth (morocco); color variations listed below. Front and back covers: blindstamped single-ruled border with $2^7/_8''$ ornament in center. Spine: goldstamped '[ornamental band] | AT HOME | AND | ABROAD. | MARGARET | FULLER | OSSOLI. | TRIBUNE | [ornamental band]'. Flyleaves. Green endpapers. All edges trimmed.

1. Dark brown cloth.
   Locations: InU, JM, MiU, NSbSU, OCIW, PHC, TxDW.
2. Dark reddish orange cloth.
   Location: InIB.
3. Green cloth.
   Locations: LNHT, MH, NjNbS, OBgU.
4. Medium purple cloth.
   Locations: FU, NIC, NNMer, NSyU, VtSjA.

Publication: Price: six-volume Tribune edition of Fuller's works, $10.00 per set. Inscribed copy: InIB (7 October 1869).

A 9.1.j
Tenth printing: Boston: Roberts Brothers, 1874.

Title page states that this is the 'New and Complete Edition'.

[1^2 2–20^{12} 21^6]

Contents: Same as in the first printing, except: p. 467: blank.

Binding: L cloth (morocco); color variations listed below. Front and back covers: blindstamped double band with perpendicular lines. Spine: blindstamped bands with goldstamped 'MARGARET | FULLER'S | WORKS | [ornamental rule] | AT HOME | AND | ABROAD. | [ornamental rule] | R [star-like publisher's device] B'. Flyleaves. Brown endpapers. All edges trimmed.

1. Dark green cloth.
   Locations: CLSU, ICHi, IP, MWC, MdBP, Mi, OAkU.
2. Dark reddish brown cloth.
   Location: BL.
3. Dark reddish orange cloth.
   Locations: InIB, JM, MeBa, OCU, WMU, WvU.
4. Dark reddish purple cloth.
   Locations: IU, MWA.

Publication: According to the Roberts Brothers' cost books, 280 copies were printed and bound as of 1 February 1874. Mrs. Arthur B. Fuller retained the plates and received 10 percent on the retail price of each copy sold. Price: $1.50.

SUBSEQUENT PRINTINGS

A 9.1.k
Eleventh printing: Boston: Roberts Brothers, 1875.

According to the Roberts Brothers' cost books, 284 copies were printed between 24 February and 14 April 1875. Price: $1.50.

A 9.1.l
Twelfth printing: Boston: Roberts Brothers, 1890.

According to the Roberts Brothers' cost books, 80 copies were printed as of 3 March 1890.

A 9.1.m
Thirteenth printing: Boston: Roberts Brothers, 1895.

According to the Roberts Brothers' cost books, 280 copies were printed as of 18 November 1895. A second issue, with the sheets of this printing (with the Roberts Brothers title page) bound in Little, Brown and Company casings, has been noted.

A 9.1.n
Fourteenth printing: Port Washington, N.Y.: Kennikat Press, 1971.

Facsimile of the 1856 text. 525 copies printed. Published February 1971.

A 10.1.a
Only edition, first printing (1860)

LIFE WITHOUT AND LIFE WITHIN;

OR,

Rebiews, Narratibes, Essays, and Poems,

BY

MARGARET FULLER OSSOLI,

AUTHOR OF "WOMAN IN THE NINETEENTH CENTURY," "AT HOME AND
ABROAD," "ART, LITERATURE, AND THE DRAMA," ETC.

EDITED BY HER BROTHER,

ARTHUR B. FULLER.

————

BOSTON:
BROWN, TAGGARD AND CHASE.
NEW YORK: SHELDON & CO.   PHILADELPHIA: J. B. LIPPINCOTT & CO.
LONDON: SAMPSON LOW, SON & CO.
1860.

A 10.1.a: 7⁹/₁₆″ × 4³/₄″

Two issues have been noted.

A 10.1.a¹
First issue

[1–2] 3–70 [71] 72–355 [356] 357–424

[1]–35⁶ 36²

Contents: Tipped-in frontispiece facing title page: romanticized version of Fuller's face from portrait by Hicks; p. 1: title page; p. 2: 'Entered, according to Act of Congress, in the year 1859, by | ARTHUR B. FULLER, | In the Clerk's Office of the District Court of the District of Massachusetts. | STEREOTYPED AT THE | BOSTON STEREOTYPE FOUNDRY. | RIVERSIDE, CAMBRIDGE: | PRINTED BY H. O. HOUGHTON AND COMPANY.'; pp. 3–8: 'PREFACE.'; pp. 9–12: contents; pp. 13–22: 'Part I. Reviews. Menzel's View of Goethe'; pp. 23–60: 'Goethe'; pp. 61–68: 'Thomas Hood'; pp. 69–70: 'Letters from a Landscape Painter'; pp. 71–82: 'Beethoven'; pp. 83–86: 'Brown's Novels'; pp. 87–92: 'Edgar A. Poe'; pp. 93–101: 'Alfieri and Cellini'; pp. 102–107: 'Italy.— Cary's Dante'; pp. 108–109: 'American Facts'; pp. 110–115: 'Napoleon and His Marshals'; pp. 116–120: 'Physical Education'; pp. 121–126: 'Frederick Douglass'; pp. 127–140: 'Philip van Artevelde'; pp. 141–142: 'United States Exploring Expedition'; pp. 143–148: 'Story-Books for the Hot Weather'; pp. 149–152: 'Shelley's Poems'; pp. 153–157: 'Festus'; pp. 158–168: 'French Novelists of the Day'; pp. 169–173: 'The New Science, or the Philosophy of Mesmerism or Animal Magnetism'; pp. 174–178: 'Deutsche Schnellpost'; pp. 179–190: 'Oliver Cromwell'; pp. 191–198: 'Emerson's Essays'; pp. 199–206: 'Capital Punishment'; pp. 207–218: 'Part II. Miscellanies. First of January'; pp. 219–225: 'New Year's Day'; pp. 226–231: 'St. Valentine's Day'; pp. 232–235: 'Fourth of July'; pp. 236–242: 'First of August'; pp. 243–249: 'Thanksgiving'; pp. 250–257: 'Christmas'; pp. 258–276: 'Mariana'; pp. 277–282: 'Sunday Meditations on Various Texts'; pp. 283–286: 'Appeal for an Asylum for Discharged Female Convicts'; pp. 287–296: 'The Rich Man. An Ideal Sketch.'; pp. 297–303: 'The Poor Man. An Ideal Sketch.'; pp. 304–307: 'The Celestial Empire'; pp. 308–313: 'Klopstock and Meta'; pp. 314–318: 'What Fits a Man to Be a Voter? A Fable.'; pp. 319–321: 'Discoveries'; pp. 322–325: 'Politeness Too Great a Luxury to Be Given to the Poor'; pp. 326–329: 'Cassius M. Clay'; pp. 330–336: 'The Magnolia of Lake Pontchartrain'; pp. 337–343: 'Consecration of Grace Church'; pp. 344–347: 'Late Aspirations. Letter to H———.'; pp. 348–353: 'Fragmentary Thoughts from Margaret Fuller's Journal'; pp. 354–355: 'Farewell'; p. 356: blank; p. 357: 'Part III. Poems. Freedom and Truth. To a Friend.'; pp. 357–361: 'Description of a Portion of the Journey to Trenton Falls'; pp. 361–365: 'Journey to Trenton Falls'; pp. 365–367: 'Sub Rosa, Crux'; pp. 367–368: 'The Dahlia, The Rose, and the Heliotrope'; pp. 368–369: 'To My Friends. Translated from Schiller.'; p. 370: 'Stanzas. Written at the Age of Seventeen.'; p. 371: 'Flaxman'; pp. 371–373: 'Thoughts on Sunday Morning, When Prevented by a Snow Storm from Going to Church'; p. 374: 'To a Golden Heart Worn Round the Neck'; pp. 375–376: 'Lines Accompanying a Bouquet of Wild Columbine, Which Bloomed Late in the Season'; pp. 377–378: 'Dissatisfaction. Translated from Theodore Körner.'; p. 378: 'My Seal-Ring'; pp. 379–380: 'The Consolers. Translated from Goethe.'; p. 380: 'Absence of Love'; pp. 381–383: 'Meditations'; pp. 383–384: 'Richter'; p. 384: 'The Thankful and the Thankless'; p. 385: 'Prophecy and Fulfilment'; pp. 385–386: 'Verses Given to W.C. with a Blank Book, March, 1844'; pp. 387–388: 'Eagles and Doves. Goethe.'; p. 388: 'To a Friend, with Heartsease'; pp. 389–390: 'Aspiration. Lines Written in the Journal of Her Brother, R.F.F.'; pp. 390–393: 'The One in All'; p. 393: 'A Greeting'; p. 394: 'Lines to Edith, On Her Birthday'; pp. 395–396: 'Lines Written in Her Brother R.F.F.'s Journal'; pp. 396–397: 'On a Picture Representing the Descent from the Cross. By Raphael.';

pp. 397–400: 'The Captured Wild Horse'; pp. 400–403: 'Epilogue to the Tragedy of Essex. Spoken in the Character of the Queen.—Translated from Goethe.'; pp. 404–405: 'Hymn Written for a Sunday School'; pp. 405–406: 'Desertion. Translation of One of Garcilaso's Eclogues.'; pp. 406–408: 'Song Written for a May Day Festival'; p. 409: 'Caradori Singing'; pp. 409–410: 'Lines in Answer to Stanzas Containing Several Passages of Distinguished Beauty, Addressed to Me By ———'; pp. 410–411: 'Influence of the Outward'; pp. 411–413: 'To Miss R.B.'; p. 413: 'Sistrum'; p. 414: 'Imperfect Thoughts'; pp. 414–416: 'Sadness'; pp. 416–417: 'Lines Written in an Album'; pp. 417–420: 'To S.C.'; pp. 420–421: 'Lines Written in Boston on a Beautiful Autumnal Day'; pp. 422–424: 'To E.C. With Herbert's Poems'.

Typography and paper: $7^9/_{16}'' \times 4^3/_4''$; wove paper; 35 lines per page. Running heads: rectos: pp. 5–7: 'PREFACE.'; p. 11: 'CONTENTS.'; pp. 15–355: titles of selections; pp. 359–423: 'POEMS.'; versos: pp. 4–8: 'PREFACE.'; pp. 10–12: 'CONTENTS.'; pp. 14–424: 'LIFE WITHOUT AND LIFE WITHIN.'.

Binding: Black S cloth (fine-ribbed). Front and back covers: blindstamped triple-ruled border with $3^3/_4''$ ornament in center. Spine: blindstamped bands and single filigree design with goldstamped variations listed below. Flyleaves. Yellow endpapers. All edges trimmed.

1. 'LIFE WITHOUT | AND | LIFE WITHIN | [rule] | MARGARET FULLER | BROWN, TAGGARD & CHASE'.
   Locations: CLSU, CSmH, CaSSU, JM, MHi, MNoW, MWalB, OBgU, VtMiM, WMM.
2. Same as no. 1, except: 'BROWN & TAGGARD' at bottom.
   Locations: ICRC, MH, MWA, MWat, MeB, OU.
3. 'MARGARET | FULLER'S | WORKS | [rule] | LIFE WITHOUT | AND | LIFE WITHIN | BROWN, TAGGARD & CHASE'.
   Locations: IEN, MA.

Publication: Announced as "will soon be issued" in *Bookseller's Medium and Publisher's Circular,* 15 October 1859, p. 98. Advertised as "Now Ready" in *Bookseller's Medium and Publisher's Circular,* 16 January 1860, p. 218, and 1 February 1860, p. 244. Announced as "in press" in *Mt. Auburn Memorial,* 1 (9 November 1859), 173. Advertised as "Ready on Jan. 11TH" in *Boston Daily Evening Transcript,* 9 January 1860, p. 3, and *Boston Daily Advertiser,* 11 January 1860, p. 2. Listed in *American Publishers' Circular and Literary Gazette,* 14 January 1860, p. 17.

A 10.1.a²
Second issue: London: Sampson Low, Son & Co., 1860.

American sheets (with first-issue title page) in English casings of green cloth. Spine: goldstamped 'LIFE WITHOUT | AND | LIFE WITHIN | [rule] | OSSOLI | [rule] | LONDON. | SAMPSON LOW, SON & CO.'.

Locations: BRU, CtY.

Publication: Advertised as "This day published" in *Publishers' Register and Booksellers' Circular,* 23 (1 February 1860), 78, and *Athenæum,* no. 1684 (4 February 1860), 155. Listed as published between 1 and 14 February in *Publishers' Register and Booksellers' Circular,* 23 (15 February 1860), 98. Price: 7s. 6d.

A 10.1.b
Second printing (1860)

Two issues have been noted.

A 10.1.b¹
First issue: Boston: Brown, Taggard and Chase; New York: Sheldon & Co.; Philadelphia: J. B. Lippincott & Co.; London: Sampson Low, Son & Co., [n.d.].

Binding: Black S cloth (fine-ribbed). Spine: goldstamping variations listed below.

1. 'LIFE WITHOUT | AND | LIFE WITHIN | [rule] | MARGARET FULLER | BROWN, TAGGARD & CHASE'.
   Locations: CCC, JM, MDeeP, MWay, MiU, NhM, RHi, ViU.
2. Same as above, except 'BROWN & TAGGARD' at bottom.
   Location: NNC.

Publication: Inscribed copies: RPB (16 January 1860), NNC (23 January 1860).

A 10.1.b²
Second issue: London: Sampson Low, Son & Co., [n.d].

American sheets (with first-issue title page) in English casings of green cloth. Spine: goldstamped 'LIFE WITHOUT | AND | LIFE WITHIN | [rule] | OSSOLI | [rule] | LONDON. | SAMPSON LOW, SON & CO.'.

Locations: BEU, BL.

Publication: Inscribed copy: BL (deposit copy, 9 November 1860).

A 10.1.c
Third printing: New York: The Tribune Association, 1869.

[1–17¹² 18⁸]

Binding: L cloth (morocco); color variations listed below. Front and back covers: blindstamped single-ruled border with 2⅞" ornament in center. Spine: goldstamped '[ornamental band] | LIFE | WITHOUT | AND | LIFE | WITHIN. | MARGARET | FULLER | OSSOLI. | TRIBUNE | [ornamental band]'. Flyleaves. Green endpapers. All edges trimmed.

1. Dark brown cloth.
   Locations: NSbSU, NbL, OCIW, PHC, TU.
2. Dark reddish orange cloth.
   Locations: In, MU, OKentU.
3. Green cloth.
   Locations: CU-D, JM, LNHT.
4. Medium purple cloth.
   Locations: JM, KMK, NNMer, NSyU, OMC.

Publication: Price: six-volume Tribune edition of Fuller's works, $10.00 per set. Inscribed copy: NbL (1 September 1869).

A 10.1.d
Fourth printing: Boston: Roberts Brothers, 1874.

[1–18¹²]

Contents: Same as in the first printing, except: pp. 425–432: advertisements for Roberts Brothers publications.

Binding: L cloth (morocco); color variations listed below. Front and back covers: blindstamped double band with perpendicular lines. Spine: blindstamped bands with goldstamped 'MARGARET | FULLER'S | WORKS | [ornamental rule] | LIFE WITHOUT

| AND | LIFE WITHIN. | [ornamental rule] | R [star-like publisher's device] B'. Fly-leaves. Brown endpapers. All edges trimmed.

1. Dark green cloth.
   Locations: MWC, MdBJ, MdBP, NcGU, NcWsW, OAkU.
2. Dark reddish brown cloth.
   Locations: BL, CLSU.
3. Dark reddish orange cloth.
   Locations: InU, JM, MWalB, MeBa, MoSW, WMU.
4. Dark reddish purple cloth.
   Locations: ICM, MWA.

Publication: According to the Roberts Brothers' cost books, 280 copies were printed and bound as of 1 February 1874. Mrs. Arthur B. Fuller retained the plates and received 10 percent on the retail price of each copy sold. Price: $1.50. Inscribed copy: NBu [rebound] (April 1874).

SUBSEQUENT PRINTINGS

A 10.1.e
Fifth printing: Boston: Roberts Brothers, 1875.

According to the Roberts Brothers' cost books, 208 copies were printed between 24 February and 14 April 1875. Price: $1.50.

A 10.1.f
Sixth printing: Boston: Roberts Brothers, 1890.

According to the Roberts Brothers' cost books, 80 copies were printed as of 13 March 1890.

A 10.1.g
Seventh printing: Boston: Roberts Brothers, 1895.

According to the Roberts Brothers' cost books, 80 copies were printed as of 8 March 1895. A second issue, with the sheets of this printing (with the Roberts Brothers title page) bound in Little, Brown and Company casings, has been noted.

A 10.1.h
Eighth printing: Upper Saddle River, N.J.: Literature House, 1970.

Facsimile of the 1860 text.

A 11 MARGARET AND HER FRIENDS

A 11.1.a
Only edition, first printing (1895)

MARGARET AND HER FRIENDS

OR

𝕮𝖊𝖓 𝕮𝖔𝖓𝖛𝖊𝖗𝖘𝖆𝖙𝖎𝖔𝖓𝖘

WITH

MARGARET FULLER

UPON

THE MYTHOLOGY OF THE GREEKS AND
ITS EXPRESSION IN ART

HELD AT THE HOUSE OF THE REV. GEORGE RIPLEY
BEDFORD PLACE, BOSTON

BEGINNING MARCH 1, 1841

REPORTED BY CAROLINE W. HEALEY

BOSTON
ROBERTS BROTHERS
1895

A 11.1.a: 7¹¹/₁₆″ × 5¹/₈″

[i–ii] [1–5] 6–15 [16–17] 18–22 [23–25] 26–39 [40] 41–59 [60] 61–76 [77] 78–94 [95] 96–105 [106] 107–122 [123] 124–134 [135] 136–146 [147] 148–155 [156] 157–162

[1–10⁸ 11²]

Contents: p. i: 'MARGARET AND HER FRIENDS'; p. ii: advertisement for four other books by Mrs. Dall published by Roberts Brothers; p. 1: title page; p. 2: '*Copyright, 1895,* | BY ROBERTS BROTHERS. | [rule] | *All rights reserved.* | UNIVERSITY PRESS: | JOHN WILSON AND SON, CAMBRIDGE, U.S.A.'; p. 3: contents; p. 4: blank; pp. 5–15: 'PREFACE.' signed 'CAROLINE HEALEY DALL. | Sept. 1, 1895, | WASHINGTON, D.C.'; p. 16: blank; pp. 17–22: members of the class; p. 23: ' "*Only a signal shown, and a distant voice in* | *the darkness.*"—LONGFELLOW.'; p. 24: blank; pp. 25–162: text.

Typography and paper: 7¹¹/₁₆″ × 5⅛″; laid paper with 1³/₁₆″ vertical chain lines; 22 lines per page. Running heads: rectos: pp. 7–15: '*PREFACE.*'; pp. 19–21: '*MEMBERS OF THE CLASS.*'; pp. 27–161: '*MARGARET AND HER FRIENDS.*'; versos: pp. 6–14: '*PREFACE.*'; pp. 18–22: '*MEMBERS OF THE CLASS.*'; pp. 26–162: '*MARGARET AND HER FRIENDS.*'.

Binding: S cloth (diagonal fine-ribbed); color variations listed below. Front cover: goldstamped 'MARGARET | AND | HER FRIENDS | [rule] | CAROLINE H. DALL', with daisy (gold center, white petals) to the left. Back cover: blank. Spine: goldstamped 'MARGARET | AND HER | FRIENDS | Caroline Healey Dall | [publisher's device of intertwined 'R' and 'B']'. Laid flyleaves. White endpapers. All edges trimmed.

1. Dark gray brown cloth.
   Locations: CoU, ICRC, MA, MC, NNC, ViU.
2. Dark olive green cloth.
   Locations: CSmH, CaOLU, DLC, Ia-T, IaDmD, MCR-S, MLen, MeL, MeP, MnHi, MnU, MoU, NIC, NbU, NcRS, PPD, RPA.
3. Gray cloth.
   Locations: ArU, CtW, DeU, ICN, IU, JM, KPT, MSa, MW, MWH, NRU, NcWsW, OO, OT, OU.
4. Light olive green cloth.
   Locations: JM, MHi, OrP, PPD, PU.
5. Medium yellow brown cloth.
   Locations: CtY, MB, MHarF, MMal, MNan, MWH, NBu, NNMer.

Publication: According to the Roberts Brothers' cost books, 600 copies were printed as of 3 October 1895. Mrs. Dall received 15 percent on the retail price of each copy sold. Advertised with "Some October Books" in *Publishers' Weekly,* 48 (19 October 1895), 691. Listed in *Publishers' Weekly,* 48 (21 December 1895), 1179. Price: $1.00. Inscribed copies: NcRS (October 1895), ViU (2 November 1895), DLC (12 November 1895), CaOLU (December 1895).

A 11.1.b
Second printing: Boston: Roberts Brothers, 1897.

The following revisions were made:

[i.15] 1895 [1897
[3.6] R.W.E. PRESENT [(R.W.E. present.)
[3.9–10] R.W.E. | PRESENT [(R.W.E. present.)
[3.12] HOAR [HOAR. (R.W.E. present.)
[3.14–15] R.W.E. | PRESENT [(R.W.E. | present.)
[3.18] V. and [V. VI. and

[3.23] [not present] [He was present at four.
21.10   W.   [DAVID

21.13–14   The family is, I think, extinct, un- | less Mrs. Stillman left a daughter. [
            She left two daughters, who are | married and have children.

Binding: S cloth (diagonal fine-ribbed); color variations listed below. Front cover
stamping same as in the first printing except for variations listed below. Spine: same
as in the first printing except for variations in publisher's device listed below.

1. Light green cloth; front cover: daisy not present; spine: publisher's device not
    present.
    Location: JM.
2. Medium yellow brown cloth; front cover: daisy present; spine: goldstamped pub-
    lisher's device of intertwined 'R' and 'B' at bottom.
    Location: NcD.
3. Medium yellow brown cloth; front cover: daisy not present; spine: goldstamped
    publisher's device of intertwined 'R' and 'B' at bottom.
    Locations: IaU, LU, NcU.
4. Medium yellow brown cloth; front cover: daisy not present; spine: goldstamped
    publisher's device of elongated 'B' through normal 'R' at bottom.
    Locations: ArL, PPT.

Publication: According to the Roberts Brothers' cost books, 280 copies were printed
as of 28 April 1897.

Note: For a full discussion of the composition and printing history, see Joel Myerson,
"Mrs. Dall Edits Miss Fuller: The Story of *Margaret and Her Friends*," *Papers of the
Bibliographical Society of America,* 72 (II Quarter 1978).

SUBSEQUENT PRINTING

A 11.1.c
Third printing: New York: Arno Press, 1972.

Facsimile of the 1895 text.

A 12.1.a
Only edition, first printing (1903)

LOVE-LETTERS OF MARGARET FULLER

1845–1846

WITH AN INTRODUCTION BY
JULIA WARD HOWE

TO WHICH ARE ADDED THE REMINISCENCES OF
RALPH WALDO EMERSON, HORACE GREELEY
AND CHARLES T. CONGDON

NEW YORK
D. APPLETON AND COMPANY
1903

A 12.1.a¹: 7¹/₂″ × 5¹/₈″

Two issues have been noted.

A 12.1.a¹
First issue

[i–iv] v–xvi 1 [2] 3–7 [8] 9–190 [191–192] 193 [194] 195–228 [229–232]

[1]–15⁸ 16⁴

Contents: p. i: 'LOVE-LETTERS | OF MARGARET FULLER'; p. ii: blank; tipped-in frontispiece facing title page: 'Redrawn from a portrait on wood, printed in Greeley's Recollections of a Busy Life.'; p. iii: title page; p. iv: 'COPYRIGHT, 1903 | BY D. APPLETON AND COMPANY | *Published June, 1903*'; pp. v–xii: 'INTRODUCTION' signed 'JULIA WARD HOWE. | BOSTON, MAY 25, 1903.'; pp. xiii–xvi: contents; p. 1: 'PREFATORY NOTE'; p. 2: blank; pp. 3–6: 'PREFATORY NOTE' *'Written in the summer of 1873, by James Gotendorf, formerly James Nathan'*; p. 7: 'THE LETTERS'; p. 8: blank; pp. 9–186: text; pp. 187–190: editorial notes; p. 191: facsimile of Fuller's letter of 14 March 1845; p. 192: blank; p. 193: 'REMINISCENCES'; p. 194: blank; pp. 195–207: 'BY RALPH WALDO EMERSON' from *Memoirs of Margaret Fuller Ossoli;* pp. 208–222: 'BY HORACE GREELEY' from his *Recollections of a Busy Life;* pp. 223–228: 'BY CHARLES T. CONGDON' from his *Reminiscences of a Journalist;* pp. 229–232: advertisements for D. Appleton publications.

Typography and paper: 7¹/₂″ × 5¹/₈″; wove paper; 25 lines per page. Running heads: rectos: pp. v–227: *'Love-Letters of Margaret Fuller';* versos: pp. vi–228: *'Love-Letters of Margaret Fuller'.*

Binding: Buckram; color variations listed below. Front cover: stamped *'LOVE LET-TERS | OF | MARGARET FULLER | [rule] | INTRODUCTION | BY | JULIA WARD HOWE'* within 4″ oval ornament; color variations listed below. Back cover: blank. Spine: stamped *'LOVE | LETTERS | OF | MARGARET | FULLER | [rule] | Apple-ton's';* color variations listed below. White endpapers. Only top and bottom edges trimmed; variations in edge-gilting listed below.

1. Brown buckram; front and spine: goldstamping; edges not gilt.
   Locations: AB, NNStJ, OkU.
2. Salmon buckram; front and spine: goldstamping; edges not gilt.
   Locations: DHU, IaU, MB, MGb, MSo, MWH.
3. Brown buckram; front and spine: redstamping; edges not gilt.
   Locations: CU-R, DCU, LNHT, MsHaU, NcD.
4. Salmon buckram; front and spine: redstamping; edges not gilt.
   Locations: CSmH, CaSSU, IHi, JM, LU, MHarF, MdBJ, MiD, N, NBu, NHC, NPV, NT, NdU, ODaWU, PMA, PSC, TxDN, WMU.
5. Brown buckram; front and spine: goldstamping; top edges gilt.
   Locations: ArU, AzU, CU-D, CU-S, CaAEU, CaOKQ, CaOWtU, CoU, CtY, DLC, FMU, ICM, ICN, IDeKN, InU, JM, KPT, KyLoU, MA, MMal, MMel, MNBedf, MNan, MQ, MRea, MW, MWalB, MWin, MdBE, Me, MeP, MiRochOU, MnU, MsU, NBrockU, NRU, NSbSU, NSyU, NcD, NjO, NjP, OAU, OC, OCU, OCIW, OYU, OrU, PBeL, PBm, PPA, RPA, TU, TxHuT, TxSmS, Vi, ViW, VtMiM, WaSpG.
6. Salmon buckram; front and spine: goldstamping; top edges gilt.
   Locations: CCC, CLU, CU-SC, CaBViV, CtW, ICarbS, JM, KMK, MBAt, MBU, MCR-S, MGro, MHi, MLen, MNt, MWA, MWiW, MnHi, MoSW, NBronSL, NBu, NIC, NN, NNMer, NNUT, NcU, OO, OOxM, OkS, P, PPT, RNR, TxDW, TxU, UPB, UU, ViU, WU.
7. Brown buckram; front and spine: redstamping; top edges gilt.
   Location: WM.

8. Salmon buckram; front and spine: redstamping; top edges gilt.
   Location: NbU.

Dust jacket: Cream background with green printing. Front cover: '[first 7 lines within 4″ oval ornament] *LOVE LETTERS | OF | MARGARET FULLER* | [rule] | *INTRODUC-TION | BY | JULIA WARD HOWE* | [8-line blurb from the 17 April 1903 *New York Daily Tribune,* within single-ruled box] | [double rule] | D. APPLETON AND COMPANY, Publishers, New York [all within single-ruled border]'. Back cover: biographies of Father Marquette, Daniel Boone, and Horace Greeley in Appleton's Series of Historic Lives. Spine: '[double rule] | *LOVE | LETTERS | OF | MARGARET | FULLER* | [double rule] | $1.35 net | Postage additional | [wreath device] | [double rule] | APPLETONS | [double rule]'. Front flap: blurbs for M. L. Avary, *A Virginia Girl in the Civil War.* Back flap: blurbs for E. Adam, *The Romance of My Childhood and Youth.*

Location: CtY.

Publication: Advertised as ready "Next Friday" in *Publishers' Weekly,* 63 (20 June 1903), 1403. Listed in *Publishers' Weekly,* 63 (27 June 1903), 1445. Price: $1.35. Copyright entry is 10 June 1903. Inscribed copies: DLC (deposit copy, 18 June 1903), CaOKQ (26 June 1903).

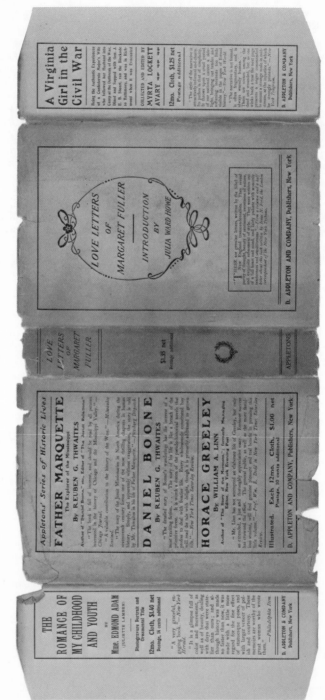

Dust jacket for A 12.1.a[1]

A 12.1.a²
Second issue: English issue of American sheets

LOVE-LETTERS OF MARGARET FULLER

1845–1846

WITH AN INTRODUCTION BY
JULIA WARD HOWE

TO WHICH ARE ADDED THE REMINISCENCES OF
RALPH WALDO EMERSON, HORACE GREELEY
AND CHARLES T. CONGDON

LONDON
T. FISHER UNWIN
11, PATERNOSTER BUILDINGS
1903

A 12.1.a²: 7¹/₂″ × 5¹/₈″

American sheets (trimmed on all edges, top edges gilt) with cancel title page in English casings of light blue buckram. Front cover: goldstamped '*LOVE | LETTERS OF | MARGARET | FULLER |* [rule] *| INTRODUCTION BY | JULIA WARD | HOWE*' within 4³/₁₆" ornate circular ornament. Back cover: blank. Spine: goldstamped '*LOVE | LETTERS | OF | MARGARET | FULLER |* [rule] | T. Fisher Unwin'.

Locations: BC, BE, BL, BLLL, BLdP, BMR, BO, BRU, CU-I, CaOTU, IU, JM, NSchU, RHi.

Publication: Listed in *Athenæum,* no. 3958 (5 September 1903), 316. Price: 5s. Inscribed copies: BL (deposit copy, 27 November 1903), BE (30 November 1903).

SUBSEQUENT PRINTINGS

A 12.1.b
Second printing: Westport, Conn.: Greenwood Press, 1969.

Facsimile of the first issue. 508 copies printed. Published 28 February 1970.

A 12.1.c
Third printing: New York: AMS Press, 1970.

Facsimile of the first issue. 300 copies printed.

A 13 THE WRITINGS OF MARGARET FULLER

A 13.1.a
Only edition, first printing (1941)

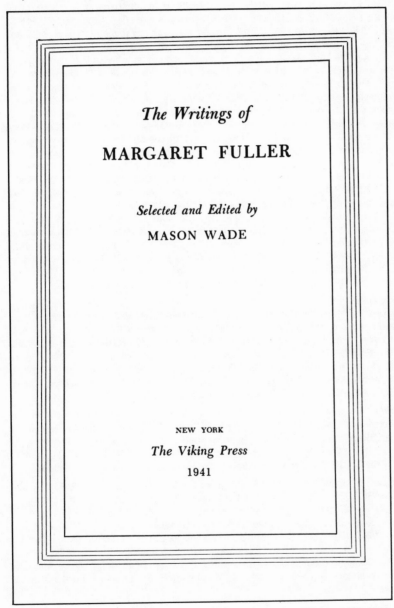

The Writings of

MARGARET FULLER

Selected and Edited by
MASON WADE

NEW YORK
The Viking Press
1941

A 13.1.a: 9¹/₄″ × 6¹/₈″

[i–iv] v–ix [x] xi [xii] [1–2] 3–104 [105–106] 107–218 [219–220] 221–403 [404–406] 407–539 [540–542] 543–592 [593–594] 595–608 [609–610]

[1–18¹⁶ 19⁸ 20¹⁶]

Contents: p. i: 'THE WRITINGS OF MARGARET FULLER'; p. ii: *'By Mason Wade |*
MARGARET FULLER: WHETSTONE OF GENIUS'; p. iii: title page; p. iv: 'COPYRIGHT
1941 BY THE VIKING PRESS, INC. | PRINTED IN U.S.A. BY THE VAIL-BALLOU PRESS
| PUBLISHED IN APRIL 1941 | *Published on the same day in the Dominion of Canada
| by The Macmillan Company of Canada Limited';* pp. v–viii: *'Introduction'* dated
'December 1940'; pp. ix–x: contents; p. xi: chronological table of Fuller's life; p. xii:
blank; p. 1: *'PART I |* Summer on the Lakes'; p. 2: blank; pp. 3–4: *'Prefatory Note';* pp.
5–104: text of *Summer on the Lakes* (1856, A 9); p. 105: *'PART II |* Woman in the
Nineteenth Century'; p. 106: blank; pp. 107–108: *'Prefatory Note';* pp. 109–218: text of
Woman in the Nineteenth Century (1855, A 8); p. 219: *'PART III |* Criticism | [13 lines
listing contents]'; p. 220: blank; pp. 221–222: *'Prefatory Note';* pp. 223–229: 'A Short
Essay on Critics'; pp. 230–231: 'Three Classes of Literature'; pp. 232–241: 'Translator's Preface to *Eckermann's Conversations with Goethe';* pp. 242–272: 'Goethe'; pp.
273–289: 'The Two Herberts'; pp. 290–300: 'Carlyle's *Cromwell';* pp. 301–311:
'French Novelists of the Day'; pp. 312–346: 'Modern British Poets'; pp. 347–357: 'Italy';
pp. 358–388: 'American Literature'; pp. 389–395: 'Emerson's Essays'; pp. 396–397:
'Poe's Tales'; pp. 398–403: 'Poe's Poems'; p. 404: blank; p. 405: *'PART IV |* Italy and
the Roman Revolution'; p. 406: blank; pp. 407–408: *'Prefatory Note';* pp. 409–539:
selections from the *New-York Tribune* letters XIII, XIV, XVI–XIX, XXI–XXXIII as printed
in *At Home and Abroad;* p. 540: blank; p. 541: *'PART V |* Letters | [25 lines listing
contents]'; p. 542: blank; p. 543: *'Prefatory Note';* pp. 544–592: texts of 25 letters; p.
593: 'Bibliography of Published Writings | of Margaret Fuller | Index'; p. 594: blank;
pp. 595–600: bibliography of Fuller's writings; pp. 601–608: index.

Typography and paper: 9¹/₄″ × 6¹/₈″; wove paper; 35 lines per page. Running heads:
rectos: p. vii: 'INTRODUCTION'; pp. 7–103: 'SUMMER ON THE LAKES'; pp. 111–217:
'WOMAN IN THE NINETEENTH CENTURY'; pp. 225–403: 'CRITICISM'; pp. 411–539:
'ITALY AND THE ROMAN REVOLUTION'; pp. 553–589: 'LETTERS'; pp. 597–599: 'BIB-
LIOGRAPHY OF PUBLISHED WRITINGS OF MARGARET FULLER'; pp. 603–607: 'IN-
DEX'; versos: pp. vi–viii: 'INTRODUCTION'; p. x: 'CONTENTS'; pp. 4–592: 'THE WRIT-
INGS OF MARGARET FULLER'; pp. 596–600: 'BIBLIOGRAPHY OF PUBLISHED WRIT-
INGS OF MARGARET FULLER'; pp. 602–608: 'INDEX'.

Binding: Medium blue green V cloth (fine linen-grained). Front cover: on upper half,
blindstamped vine over open book with 'M' and 'F' on facing pages over sword
design. Back cover: blank. Spine: blindstamped rules with goldstamped lettering: '[2
rules] | THE | WRITINGS | OF | Margaret | Fuller | BY | MASON WADE | [19 rules] |
THE VIKING | PRESS | [rule]'. Flyleaves. Cream endpapers. All edges trimmed.

Dust jacket: Cream background with green printing. Front cover: 'THE WRITINGS |
of | MARGARET | FULLER | [vine-book-sword design] | *Selected and Edited by* |
MASON WADE', within triple-ruled border, all within thick solid border. Back cover:
32-line description of book. Spine: '[thick rule] | [wavy vertical design] | [thick rule] |
The | WRITINGS | *of* | [next 2 lines in cream on a thick green rule] MARGARET |
FULLER | *Mason Wade* | [next 2 lines in cream on a thick green rule] THE | VIKING |
PRESS | [wavy vertical design] | [thick rule]'. Front flap: blurbs for M. Wade, *Margaret
Fuller: Whetstone of Genius.* Back flap: blurbs for R. M. du Gard, *The World of the
Thibaults.*

Location: JM (with dust jacket).

Publication: 2,000 copies printed. Published 21 April 1941. Price: $5.00.

THE WRITINGS
of
MARGARET
FULLER

Selected and Edited by
MASON WADE

THE WRITINGS OF
Margaret Fuller
SELECTED AND EDITED BY MASON WADE

The serious, last year, of Mason Wade's life, of the woman who was the friend of Hawthorne, Emerson, Thoreau, and Carlyle and all who will entitle in America whose influence equalled that of Edgar Allan Poe. Mr. Wade, whose research for the biography made him familiar with the literary material in its original form, has produced from it a varied and stimulating volume, redolent of the spirit of the time and the personality of the author. The reader still had here Miss Fuller's *Summer on the Lakes*, an anecdotal and thoughtful account of her journey to the then very remote American West. He will discover also Woman in the Nineteenth Century, a work of unparalleled influence in its own day and still interesting long after its battle for woman suffrage is won, for the hegemony of the argument and the richness of the allusion.

From Miss Fuller's critical writings, the editor has chosen essays that have personal interest—estimates of Goethe, Carlyle, Balzac, Walter Scott, Longfellow, Hawthorne, and Poe among others. The section of the book called "Italy and the Roman Revolution" is a collection of her letters written for publication in Greeley's *Tribune* and showing her development from native tourist to skilled propagandist and fighter for freedom. Personified here in continuous narrative, these dispatches provide the nearest approximation to the celebrated Roman Revolution, but with the author all the sheer of Pico Island.

The concluding portion of this collection contains a group of Miss Fuller's personal letters—a form of writing in which she was unrivalled. Many of these are to her friends and relatives, many to famous persons of the day, including Emerson and Mazzini.

None of Margaret Fuller's books is today in general circulation, and many of them exist only in exceedingly rare copies. This new book, restoring them to the public, contains a full bibliography and index. It is a work of invaluable scholarship as well as a volume of charming and entertaining prose.

The Viking Press · Publishers · New York City

Mason Wade

has been on the staffs of several publishing houses, is a contributor of critical articles to the New York Times, New York Herald Tribune, North American Review, New Republic, Catholic World (London), and other journals. His first book, Margaret Fuller: Whetstone of Genius, was greeted with enthusiasm by the public, and received critical acclaim so highly enthusiastic of which the extensive notices below are typical. All his present work upon a biography of Francis Park-man.

MARGARET FULLER:
Whetstone of Genius

Illustrated, $3.50

"A freshly conceived and vital picture of a fascinating and unique woman and the society in which she played a traffic great part."—CIARA GRENSEMANE STROLLMAN, New York Herald Tribune Books.

"In the account of this powerful and enigmatic personality we have what his life needed—a biography both profound and sympathetic both . . . A rich biography of one of the most distinguished American women of her time."—HENRIETTA WINGATE SMITH, Boston Transcript.

"One of the most distinguished biographies of recent years."—FLOYD B. WOLFSON, Detroit Free Press.

"Mr. Wade has told this story in detail and with a genuine understanding by it has told that his full and careful life."—New York Times.

The Viking Press
18 East 48th Street, New York City

Dust jacket for A 13.1.a

SUBSEQUENT PRINTING

A 13.1.b
Second printing: Clifton, N.J.: Augustus M. Kelley, 1973.

Facsimile of the 1941 edition. 500 copies printed. Published October 1973.

A 14 MARGARET FULLER: AMERICAN ROMANTIC

A 14.1.a
Only edition, first printing (1963)

MARGARET FULLER
AMERICAN ROMANTIC

A SELECTION FROM
HER WRITINGS AND CORRESPONDENCE

EDITED BY
PERRY MILLER

Anchor Books
Doubleday & Company, Inc.
Garden City, New York
1963

A 14.1.a: 7³/₁₆″ × 4³/₁₆″

[i–ix] x–xxviii [xxix] xxx–xxxi [xxxii–xxxiv] [1] 2–31 [32–33] 34–56 [57] 58–134 [135] 136–252 [253] 254–316 [317] 318–319 [320–326]

Perfect binding.

Contents: p. i: 'MARGARET FULLER: AMERICAN ROMANTIC | [Doubleday Anchor Books device]'; p. ii: blank; p. iii: 15-line biographical sketch of Perry Miller; p. iv: blank; p. v: title page; p. vi: 'The Anchor Books edition | is the first publication of | *Margaret Fuller: American Romantic.* | Anchor Books edition: 1963 | Library of Congress Catalog Card Number 63-13082 | Copyright © 1963 by Perry Miller | All Rights Reserved | Printed in the United States of America'; p. vii: *'Margaret had so many aspects to her soul that she | might furnish material for a hundred biographers, not all | could be said even then. | James Freeman Clarke | to Thomas Wentworth Higginson, 1883.';* p. viii: blank; pp. ix–xxviii: foreword; pp. xxix–xxxi: contents; p. xxxii: blank; p. xxxiii: 'MARGARET FULLER: AMERICAN ROMANTIC'; p. xxxiv: blank; pp. 1–31: 'CHAPTER I. CAMBRIDGE, 1810–1833'; p. 32: blank; pp. 33–56: 'CHAPTER II. GROTON, PROVIDENCE, JAMAICA PLAIN 1833–1840'; pp. 57–134: 'CHAPTER III. THE *DIAL*, 1840–1844'; pp. 135–252: 'CHAPTER IV. NEW YORK, 1844–1846'; pp. 253–316: 'CHAPTER V. EUROPE, 1846–1850'; pp. 317–319: 'BIBLIOGRAPHICAL SOURCES AND ACKNOWLEDGMENTS'; p. 320: blank; pp. 321–326: catalogue of Anchor Books.

Typography and paper: 7³/₁₆″ × 4³/₁₆″; wove paper; 37 lines per page. Running heads: rectos: pp. xi–xxvii: *'Foreword';* p. xxxi: *'Contents';* pp. 3–315: chapter titles; p. 319: *'Bibliographical Sources and Acknowledgments';* versos: pp. x–318: *'Margaret Fuller: American Romantic'.*

Binding: Brown, tan, and white stiff paper wrappers. Front wrapper divided into three parts: top section: dark brown rectangular block within tan background, 'A356' in white at upper left, '$1.45' in white at upper right, white circular form in middle with '[2 lines in crude script] Margaret | Fuller | AMERICAN | ROMANTIC' in black within; middle section: 'A Selection from Her Writings | and Correspondence | Edited and with an Introduction and Notes by | PERRY MILLER | A DOUBLEDAY ANCHOR ORIGINAL' in black on tan background; bottom section: dark brown rectangular block within tan background, Doubleday Anchor Books device in black at lower left, white circular form in middle with crude black-and-white facial portrait of Fuller within. Front wrapper, verso, and back wrapper, recto: white, blank. Back wrapper, verso: tan with '[2 lines in crude script] Margaret | Fuller | AMERICAN ROMANTIC | Edited and with an Introduction and Notes by | PERRY MILLER | [26-line description of book] | Cover design by Robert R. Wright | [Doubleday Anchor Books device at left] | A DOUBLE-DAY ANCHOR ORIGINAL' in black. Spine: tan with '[in crude script, printed vertically] MARGARET FULLER | [next 2 lines printed vertically and parallel] Edited by | PERRY MILLER | [next 3 lines printed horizontally] Anchor | A356 | [triangular device]' in black. All edges trimmed.

Location: JM.

Publication: 10,000 copies printed. Published July 1963. Price: $1.45.

SUBSEQUENT PRINTINGS

A 14.1.b
Second printing: Gloucester, Mass.: Peter Smith Publishers, 1969.

Facsimile of the Doubleday edition.

A356 $1.45

Margaret Fuller

AMERICAN
ROMANTIC

A Selection from Her Writings
and Correspondence

Edited and with an Introduction and Notes by

PERRY MILLER

A DOUBLEDAY ANCHOR ORIGINAL

Stiff printed paper wrapper for A 14.1.a

A 14.1.c
Third printing: Ithaca, N.Y.: Cornell University Press, 1970.

Stiff paper wrappers. Facsimile of the Doubleday edition. 5,252 copies printed. Published 27 March 1970.

A 15 THE WOMAN AND THE MYTH: MARGARET FULLER'S LIFE AND
   WRITINGS

A 15.1.a
Only edition, first printing [1976]

Bell Gale Chevigny

The Woman and the Myth

Margaret Fuller's Life and Writings

THE FEMINIST PRESS

A 15.1.a: 9″ × 6″

Library of Congress Cataloging in Publication Data:

Chevigny, Bell Gale.
    The woman and the myth: Margaret Fuller's life and writings.

    Includes a selection of writings by M. Fuller.
    Includes bibliographical references.

    1. Ossoli, Sarah Margaret Fuller, marchesa d', 1810-1850.
    2. Woman—Social and moral questions. I. Ossoli, Sarah
Margaret Fuller, marchesa d', 1810-1850. The woman and the
myth. 1976. II. Title.

    PS2506.C48   818'.3'09[B]   76-19030   ISBN 0-912670-43-6

Art Director/Designer: Susan Trowbridge
Assistants: Barbara Gore, Mary Mulrooney

This book was typeset in Press Roman by O.B.U., New York,
New York, with Caslon and Palatino heads supplied by
Automated Composition Service, Inc., Lancaster, Pennsylvania.
It was printed on 60 # offset by R.R. Donnelley & Sons Company,
Chicago, Illinois.

The Feminist Press gratefully acknowledges the Schlesinger
Library, Radcliffe College, for permission to reproduce
the photo of Margaret Fuller used on the cover.

First edition

[i–xviii] 1–15 [16–17] 18–63 [64–65] 66–139 [140–141] 142–207 [208–209] 210–279 [280–281] 282–363 [364–365] 366–497 [498] 499–500 [501–502]

Perfect binding.

Contents: p. i: blank; p. ii: 37-line biographical sketch of Bell Gale Chevigny; p. iii: *'In the chamber | of death, I prayed | in very early years, | "Give me truth; | cheat me by no illusion." | O, the granting of | this prayer is | sometimes terrible to me! | I walk over the | burning ploughshares, | and they sear | my feet. Yet nothing but | the truth will do. | —Margaret Fuller, | Memoirs, I, 303';* p. iv: 28-line list of the Reprints Advisory Board; p. v: title page; p. vi: copyright page; p. vii: dedication page; p. viii: blank; pp. ix–xv: contents; p. xvi: blank; p. xvii: 'The | Woman | and the | Myth | *Margaret Fuller's | Life and Writings';* p. xviii: blank; pp. 1–15: introduction; p. 16: blank; p. 17: 'PART | I | The Problem of | Identity | and Vocation'; pp. 18–63: Part I; p. 64: blank; p. 65: 'PART | II | The Friend'; pp. 66–139: Part II; p. 140: blank; p. 141: 'PART | III | The | Transcendentalist | *Teacher, Editor, Literary Critic';* pp. 142–207: Part III; p. 208: blank; p. 209: 'PART | IV | The Feminist'; pp. 210–279: Part IV; p. 280: blank; p. 281: 'PART | V | The Social Critic | and Journalist'; pp. 282–363: Part V; p. 364: blank; p. 365: 'PART | VI | The Radical | in Italy'; pp. 366–497: Part VI; p. 498: blank; pp. 499–500: chronology of Fuller's life; p. 501: about The Feminist Press; p. 502: blank.

Typography and paper: 9″ × 6″; wove paper; varying number of lines per page. Running heads: rectos: pp. 3–15, 19–29, 67–83, 143–157, 211–223, 283–303, 367–

401: 'Introduction'; pp. 31, 33, 85–93, 161–165, 225–235, 305–309, 403–421: 'Contemporaries on Fuller'; pp. 37–63, 95–139, 167–207, 239–279, 311–363, 423–497: 'Fuller's Writings'; versos: pp. 2–14: 'Introduction'; pp. 18–496: chapter titles.

Binding: Turquoise, light turquoise, black, gray, and white stiff paper wrappers. Front wrapper contains two rectangular blocks with black and white borders on turquoise background, one vertical and right of center, the other laid horizontally over the first below center; within horizontal block; '[swash 'T'] The Woman | and the Myth | *Margaret Fuller's Life and Writings*' in turquoise on light turquoise background; within vertical block, top has photograph of Fuller; bottom: 'Bell Gale Chevigny' in black on gray background; to the left of editor's name, outside blocks, '[first line printed vertically before 'F' and 'P'] THE | FEMINIST | PRESS' in white. Front wrapper, verso, and back wrapper, recto: white, blank. Back wrapper, verso: within one rectangular block with black and white borders on turquoise background, left of center, 47 lines of readers' comments in black on gray background. Spine: within one rectangular block with black and white borders on turquoise background, '[in turquoise, printed vertically] The Woman and the Myth | [next 2 lines in turquoise, printed vertically and parallel] *Margaret Fuller's | Life and Writings* | [in black, printed horizontally] CHEVIGNY | [in turquoise, printed horizontally] THE | [next 2 lines in turquoise, printed vertically and parallel] FEMINIST | PRESS' on light turquoise background. All edges trimmed and stained turquoise.

Location: JM.

Publication: 5,000 copies printed. Published 1 January 1977. Price: $6.50.

SUBSEQUENT PRINTING

A 15.1.b
Second printing: Old Westbury, N.Y.: The Feminist Press, 1977.

[i–xviii] 1–15 [16–17] 18–63 [64–65] 66–139 [140–141] 142–207 [208–209] 210–279 [280–281] 282–363 [364–365] 366–497 [498] 499–509 [510]

The major differences from the first printing are: (1) on copyright page is 'First edition, second printing'; (2) 'Index' is on pp. 501–509; (3) 'About the Feminist Press' is on p. 510. 5,000 copies printed. Published late 1977.

The Woman and the Myth

Margaret Fuller's Life and Writings

Bell Gale Chevigny

THE FEMINIST PRESS

Stiff printed paper wrapper for A 15.1.a

Margaret Fuller: Essays on American Life and Letters

Joel Myerson, *Editor*

UNIVERSITY OF SOUTH CAROLINA

COLLEGE & UNIVERSITY PRESS · *Publishers*

NEW HAVEN, CONN.

A 16: 8″ × 5³/₈″

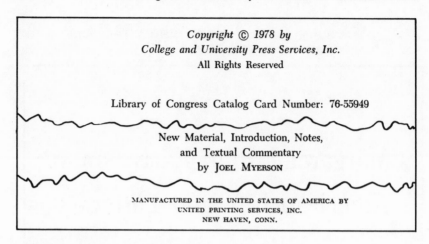

[1–6] 7–41 [42] 43–48 [49–50] 51–400

Perfect binding.

Contents: p. 1: *'The Masterworks of Literature Series* | WILLIAM S. OSBORNE, *Editor* | *Southern Connecticut State College* | *Margaret Fuller:* | *Essays on American Life and Letters';* p. 2: blank; p. 3: title page; p. 4: copyright page; pp. 5–6: 'Contents'; pp. 7–30: 'Introduction'; pp. 31–41: 'Bibliographical Note'; p. 42: blank; pp. 43–48: 'Textual Note'; p. 49: *'Margaret Fuller:* | *Essays on American Life and Letters';* p. 50: blank; pp. 51–57: 'A Short Essay on Critics'; p. 58: 'Hawthorne's *Grandfather's Chair';* p. 59: 'Lowell's *A Year's Life';* pp. 60–61: 'Hawthorne's *Twice-Told Tales';* pp. 62–81: 'From *Summer on the Lakes, in 1843';* pp. 82–239: *'Woman in the Nineteenth Century';* pp. 240–247: 'Emerson's Essays'; pp. 248–253: 'Thanksgiving'; pp. 254–260: 'Christmas'; pp. 261–266: 'New Year's Day'; pp. 267–270: 'Children's Books'; pp. 271–276: 'Etherology'; pp. 277–281: 'St. Valentine's Day—Bloomingdale Asylum for the Insane'; pp. 282–283: 'Cheap Postage Bill'; pp. 284–288: 'The Excellence of Goodness'; pp. 289–290: 'American Facts'; pp. 291–293: 'Prevalent Idea that Politeness is too great a Luxury to be given to the Poor'; pp. 294–296: 'Frederick Douglass'; pp. 297–300: 'Fourth of July'; pp. 301–302: 'Poe's *Tales';* pp. 303–310: 'The Wrongs of American Women and The Duty of American Women'; pp. 311–316: 'Poe's *The Raven and Other Poems';* pp. 317–324: *'Longfellow's Poems';* pp. 325–328: 'Cassius M. Clay'; pp. 329–337: 'The Rich Man—An Ideal Sketch'; pp. 338–348: 'Darkness Visible'; pp. 349–351: 'Consecration of Grace Church'; pp. 352–361: 'The Poor Man—An Ideal Sketch'; pp. 362–365: 'What fits a Man to be a Voter? Is it to be White Within, or White Without'; p. 366: 'Melville's *Typee';* pp. 367–370: 'Mistress of herself, though china fall'; pp. 371–374: 'Hawthorne's *Mosses from an Old Manse';* pp. 375–378: 'Brown's Novels'; pp. 379–380: 'Farewell'; pp. 381–400: 'American Literature; Its Position in the Present Time, and Prospects for the Future'.

Typography and paper: 8″ × 5³/₈″; wove paper; 42 lines per page. Running heads: rectos: pp. 9–29: *'Introduction';* pp. 33–41: *'Bibliographical Note';* pp. 45–47: *'Textual Note';* pp. 53–399: titles of selections; versos: pp. 8–400: 'MARGARET FULLER'.

Binding: Light blue, yellow, and black stiff paper wrappers. Front wrapper, top: black printing on light blue background: *'Masterworks of* [oval 'M' and 'L' device] *Literature Series'* with quill pen and ink bottle going down entire left margin; middle:

large yellow and small black rectangular forms within white border on three sides, flush right, with 'MARGARET FULLER: | ESSAYS ON AMERICAN | LIFE AND LET-TERS' in black on yellow background; bottom: black printing on light blue background: 'Joel Myerson | *Editor'*. Back wrapper: black printing on light blue background: 'MARGARET FULLER: | ESSAYS ON AMERICAN LIFE AND LETTERS | *Edited by Joel Myerson* | [20-line description of book] | *ABOUT THE EDITOR* | [12-line sketch of editor] | [rule] | [College and University Press device to the left of next 2 lines] COLLEGE AND UNIVERSITY PRESS • Publishers | 263 Chapel Street   New Haven, Conn. 06513'. Spine: black printing on light blue background: 'FULLER | [vertical] MARGARET FULLER: ESSAYS ON AMERICAN LIFE AND LETTERS | [2 lines horizontal] [College and University Press device] | M–46'. All edges trimmed.

Locations: JM, ScU.

Publication: 2,000 copies printed. Published summer 1978. Price: $3.95.

Masterworks of ML *Literature Series*

MARGARET FULLER: ESSAYS ON AMERICAN LIFE AND LETTERS

Joel Myerson

Editor

Stiff printed paper wrapper for A 16

B. Writings in Collections

B 1
Select Minor Poems, Translated from the German of Goethe and Schiller. Ed. John S. Dwight. Boston: Hilliard, Gray, 1839.

First printing of "To a Golden Heart, Worn Round His Neck" and "Eagles and Doves," translated from Goethe (pp. 31, 104–105).

B 2
Characteristics of Men of Genius; A Series of Biographical, Historical, and Critical Essays, Selected, by Permission, Chiefly from the North American Review. Vols. I, II. [Ed. John J. Chapman]. London: Chapman, Brothers, 1846.

Reprints "Goethe" and "Canova" from the *Dial* (I, 275–315, and II, 157–192).

B 3
The Rose of Sharon: A Religious Souvenir for M DCCC XLVI. Ed. Miss S. C. Edgarton. Boston: A. Tompkins and B. B. Mussey, 1846.

First printing of "During a Summer Shower, June, 1844" and "Lines Suggested by Raphael's Descent from the Cross" (pp. 151, 209–210).

B 4
Friends of Freedom. *The Liberty Bell.* Boston: Massachusetts Anti-Slavery Society, 1846.

First printing of "The Liberty Bell" (pp. 80–88).

B 5
The Prose Writers of America. Ed. Rufus Wilmot Griswold. Philadelphia: Carey and Hart, 1846.

Reprints "Niagara" from *Summer on the Lakes* (pp. 538–539).

B 6
The Female Poets of America. Ed. Rufus Wilmot Griswold. Philadelphia: Carey and Hart, 1848.

Reprints "Governor Everett Receiving the Indian Chiefs, November, 1837," "The Sacred Marriage," "Sonnets. I. Orpheus. II. Instrumental Music. III. Beethoven. IV. Mozart. V. To Allston's Picture, 'The Bride,'" "To Edith, on Her Birthday," "Lines Written in Illinois," "On Leaving the West," "Ganymede to His Eagle," "Life a Temple," "Encouragement," and "Gunhilda" from the *Dial, Summer on the Lakes,* and *Woman in the Nineteenth Century* (pp. 251–255).

B 7

The Mayflower. For M DCCC XLVIII. Ed. Mrs. E. Oakes Smith. Boston: Saxton and Kelt, 1848.

First printing of "Mary Stuart" (pp. 166–169).

B 8

The Female Prose Writers of America. Ed. John S. Hart. Philadelphia: E. H. Butler, 1851.

Reprints "A Short Essay on Critics" from the *Dial* (pp. 268–274).

B 9

The White Veil. A Bridal Gift. Ed. Sarah Josepha Hale. Philadelphia: E. H. Butler, 1854.

Reprints "The Sacred Marriage" (pp. 247–248).

B 10

The Wedding Dress. Ed. A Lady. Boston: Thomas G. Walker, 1854.

Reprints "Encouragement" (p. 69).

B 11

Duyckinck, Evert A. and George L. *Cyclopædia of American Literature.* Vol. II. New York: Charles Scribner, 1855.

Reprints "A Dialogue" (poem) from the *Dial* (pp. 527–528).

B 12

Hale, Sarah Josepha. "Sarah Margaret Fuller." In her *Woman's Record; or, Sketches of All Distinguished Women, from the Creation to A.D. 1854.* New York: Harpers, 1855.

Reprints "A Night in Michigan" and "The Prairie" from *Summer on the Lakes;* "American Women," "Love," "True Marriage," and "Female Progress" from *Woman in the Nineteenth Century;* "On Leaving the West"; and "The Sacred Marriage" (pp. 667–670).

B 13

Anon. *How to Write: A Pocket Manual of Composition and Letter-Writing.* New York: Fowler and Wells, 1856.

Reprints letters to her sister, 19 June 1849; to her mother, 14 May 1850; and to Richard Fuller, 19 January 1849.

B 14

The Harp and the Cross. A Collection of Religious Poetry. Comp. Stephen G. Bulfinch. Boston: American Unitarian Association, 1857.

Reprints "I will not leave you Comfortless," originally "Lines Written in March, 1836," from *Woman in the Nineteenth Century, and Kindred Papers* (pp. 82–85).

B 15

A Gallery of Distinguished English and American Female Poets. Ed. Henry Coppée. Philadelphia: E. H. Butler, 1860.

Reprints "Instrumental Music," "To Edith, on Her Birthday," and "Life a Temple" (pp. 303–307).

B 16
[Kennedy, John Pendleton, and Bliss, Alexander]. *Autograph Leaves of Our Country's Authors*. Baltimore: Cushings & Bailey, 1864.

Facsimile printing of holograph "Lines written in her Brother's Journal," first printed as "Life a Temple" (pp. 180–181).

B 17
Golden Leaves from the American Poets. Ed. John W. S. Howe. New York: Bunce and Huntington, 1865.

Reprints "Ganymede to His Eagle" (pp. 181–185).

B 18
Lyra Americana; or, Verses of Praise and Faith, from American Poets. Ed. George T. Rider. New York: D. Appleton, 1865.

Reprints "The Christ Child," a revised version of "Hymn Written for a Sunday School," from *Life Without and Life Within* (pp. 130–131).

B 19
Martin, Benj. M. *Choice Specimens of American Literature*. New York: Sheldon, 1871.

Reprints "The Real Subordinate to the Ideal" and "Character of Carlyle" from the *Memoirs* (p. 119).

B 20
Underwood, Francis H. *A Hand-Book of English Literature. American Authors*. Boston: Lee and Shepard, 1872.

Reprints "Scott and Burns" and "Carlyle" from *At Home and Abroad* (pp. 336–338).

B 21
Martin, Benj. M. *Choice Specimens of American Literature, and Literary Reader*. 2nd ed., rev. and improved. New York: Sheldon, 1875.

Reprints "Character of Carlyle" from *At Home and Abroad* (pp. 255–256).

B 22
A Century of American Literature 1776–1876. Ed. Henry A. Beers. New York: Henry Holt, 1878.

Reprints "Rock River and Oregon," "Ganymede to His Eagle," and "The Western Eden" from *Summer on the Lakes* (pp. 262–276).

B 23
Poetry of America. Ed. W. J. Linton. London: George Bell, 1878.

Reprints "The Temple of Life" (i.e., "Life a Temple") (pp. 129–130).

B 24
Poems of Places. America. Western States. Ed. Henry W. Longfellow. Boston: Houghton, Osgood, 1879.

Reprints "Lines Written in Illinois" (pp. 15–16).

B 25
Ballou, Maturin M. *Notable Thoughts About Women*. Boston: Houghton, Mifflin, 1882.

Prints 21 brief comments from Fuller's writings (pp. 14, 22, 38, 42, 90, 131, 172, 173, 175–178, 180, 233, 237, 244, 268, 323, 360).

B 26
Milburn, W. H. *The Royal Gallery of Poetry and Art.* New York: N. D. Thompson, 1887.

Reprints "On Leaving the West" (p. 312).

B 27
"Sarah Margaret Fuller Ossoli." In *A Library of American Literature from the Earliest Settlement to the Present Time.* Vol. VI. Ed. Edmund Clarence Stedman and Ellen Mackay Hutchinson. New York: Charles L. Webster, 1888.

Reprints "Men and Women" from *Woman in the Nineteenth Century,* "The True Criticism" from *Papers on Literature and Art,* and "Rachel" from a letter dated 1847 in the *Memoirs* (pp. 520–527).

B 28
Ladies of the First Unitarian Church of Oakland, California. *Borrowings.* San Francisco: C. A. Murdock, 1889.

Brief quotes from Fuller (pp. 10, 30).

B 29
American Sonnets. Ed. William Sharp. London: Walter Scott, [1889].

Reprints "Orpheus" (p. 170).

B 30
Representative Sonnets by American Poets. Ed. Charles H. Crandall. Boston: Houghton, Mifflin, 1890.

Reprints "Orpheus" (p. 250).

B 31
American Sonnets. Ed. T. W. Higginson and E. H. Bigelow. Boston: Houghton, Mifflin, 1890.

Reprints "Beethoven" (p. 169).

B 32
More Borrowings. Comp. Ladies of the First Unitarian Church of Oakland, California. San Francisco: C. A. Murdock, 1891.

Reprints an epigram from Fuller (p. 45).

B 33
A Library of the World's Best Literature Ancient and Modern. Vol. XV. Ed. Charles Dudley Warner. New York: International Society, 1897.

Reprints "George Sand" from a letter to E. Hoar in the *Memoirs,* "Americans Abroad in Europe" from *At Home and Abroad,* and "A Character Sketch of Carlyle" from a letter to Emerson in the *Memoirs* (pp. 6123–6128).

B 34
Woman in Epigram. Flashes of Wit, Wisdom, and Satire from the World's Literature. Comp. Frederick W. Morton. Chicago: A. C. McClurg, 1899.

Reprints an epigram from *Woman in the Nineteenth Century* (p. 199).

B 35
Classic Memoirs. The World's Great Classics, ed. Justin McCarthy et. al. New York: Colonial Press, 1901.

Reprints, as "Sojourn in Rome," letters and journal entries beginning in March 1849 from the *Memoirs* (pp. 341–384).

B 36
The First Number of the Dial. Old South Leaflets, 137. Boston: Old South Leaflets, 1903.

Reprints "A Short Essay on Critics" (pp. 4–10).

B 37
The Poets of Transcendentalism: An Anthology. Ed. George Willis Cooke. Boston: Houghton, Mifflin, 1903.

Reprints "Life a Temple," "Encouragement," and "Sub Rosa, Crux" from *Life Without and Life Within;* and incorrectly attributes "Dryad Song" to Fuller (pp. 75–84).

B 38
American Literary Criticism. Ed. William Morton Payne. London: Longmans, Green, 1904.

Reprints "A Short Essay on Critics" and "American Literature" from *Papers on Literature and Art* (pp. 129–157).

B 39
The Best of the World's Classics. Vol. X. Ed. Henry Cabot Lodge and Francis W. Halsey. New York: Funk & Wagnalls, 1909.

Reprints, as "Her Visit to George Sand," letter of 18 January 1847 to E. Hoar and, as "Two Glimpses of Carlyle," letter of 16 November 1846 to Emerson from the *Memoirs* (pp. 52–57).

B 40
Braun, Frederick Augustus. *Margaret Fuller and Goethe.* New York: Henry Holt, 1910.

First printing of "Eins und Alles," translated from Goethe, and "Dauer Im Wechsel," imitated from Goethe, and first complete printing of "A Credo" (1842), all edited from manuscript (pp. 231–233, 248–257).

B 41
Women as Letter-Writers. Ed. Ada M. Ingpen. New York: Baker and Taylor, 1912.

Reprints letters of 1837? on Fanny Kemble, of 25 November 1843 on Beethoven, of 16 November 1846 to Emerson on Carlyle, of December 1846 to Emerson on Carlyle, of 18 January 1847 to E. Hoar on George Sand, of 1847 to E. Hoar, of 1 December 1849 to her mother on Angelo, and of 14 May 1850 to her mother from the *Memoirs* (pp. 385–402).

B 42
Sunlit Days. Comp. Florence Hobard Perin. Boston: Little, Brown, 1915.

Reprints, without title, "I am immortal! I know it! I feel it!" (p. 264).

B 43
Historic Mackinac. Vol. II. Ed. Edwin O. Wood. New York: Macmillan, 1918.

Reprints selections from *Summer on the Lakes* (pp. 362–376).

B 44
Dow, Charles Mason. *Anthology and Bibliography of Niagara Falls.* Vol. I. Albany: J. B. Lyon, 1921.

Reprints letter of 10 June 1843 from *Summer on the Lakes* (pp. 234–240).

B 45
American Poetry and Prose: A Book of Readings 1607–1916. Ed. Norman Foerster. Boston: Houghton Mifflin, 1925.

Reprints "Richter" from *Life Without and Life Within* (pp. 484–485).

B 46
The Literature of America. Vol. I, *From the Beginning to the Civil War.* Ed. Arthur Hobson Quinn, Albert Croll Baugh, and Will David Howe. New York: Scribners, 1929.

Reprints "On a Picture Representing the Descent from the Cross by Raphael" (p. 420).

B 47
The Lost Art: Letters of Seven Famous Women. Ed. Dorothy Van Doren. New York: Coward-McCann, 1929.

Reprints letters of 16 August 1846 to her mother, to C. Sturgis on Mazzini and Wordsworth, of 20 June 1847 to Emerson, of 29 October 1847 to her brother Richard, of 16 December 1847 to her mother, of 20 December 1847 to Emerson, of 1 April 1848 to Emerson, of 29 March 1849 to Emerson, of 9 March 1849 to Marcus Spring, of 10 June 1849 to Emerson, of 8 July 1849 to her brother Richard, to her mother of July 1849, of ca. July 1849 to Ellen Fuller Channing, of 7 November 1849 to her mother, of 1 December 1849 to her mother, and of 14 May 1850 to her mother from the *Memoirs* (pp. 285–315).

B 48
The Romantic Triumph: American Literature from 1830 to 1860. Ed. Tremaine McDowell. New York: Macmillan, 1933.

Reprints "Man versus Woman" from *Woman in the Nineteenth Century* and "Aspiration" from *Life Without and Life Within* (pp. 289–291).

B 49
American Poetry and Prose. Part I, *To the Civil War.* Ed. Norman Foerster. Rev. and enlarged ed. Boston: Houghton Mifflin, 1934.

Reprints "A Dialogue. Poet. Critic." and a review of Carlyle's *Heroes and Hero-Worship* from the *Dial* (pp. 627–630).

B 50
Haraszti, Zoltán. *The Idyll of Brook Farm as Revealed by Unpublished Letters In the Boston Public Library.* 2nd ed., enlarged. Boston: Trustees of the Public Library, 1940.

First complete printing of poem beginning, "To the lone prophet of an earlier age" (pp. 26–27).

B 51

The Democratic Spirit: A Collection of American Writings from the Earliest Times to the Present Day. Ed. Bernard Smith. New York: Knopf, 1941.

Reprints "Poets of the People" from the *Tribune* and a selection from *Woman in the Nineteenth Century* (pp. 294–299).

B 52

World's Great Love Letters. Sel. Robert Sherman. Cleveland: World, 1943.

Reprints letter of 25 November 1843 on Beethoven (pp. 178–180).

B 53

American Issues. Vol. I, *The Social Record.* Ed. Willard Thorp, Merle Curti, and Carlos Baker. Philadelphia: J. B. Lippincott, 1944.

Reprints a selection from *Woman in the Nineteenth Century* (pp. 462–464).

B 54

Discovery of Europe. Ed. Philip Rahv. Boston: Houghton Mifflin, 1947.

Reprints three *Tribune* letters: 18 October 1847, n.d. (no. XVIII), and 27 May 1849 (pp. 161–172).

B 55

American Literature: An Anthology and Critical Survey. Vol. I. Ed. Joe Lee Davis, John T. Frederick, and Frank Luther Mott. New York: Scribners, 1948.

Reprints "The Principle of Liberty" from *Woman in the Nineteenth Century* (pp. 640–641).

B 56

An American Treasury. Ed. Hugh Graham. Chicago: Peoples Book Club, 1949.

Reprints brief epigrams from Fuller (pp. 253, 278, 279).

B 57

The Romantic Triumph: American Literature from 1830 to 1860. Ed. Tremaine McDowell. Rev. ed. New York: Macmillan, 1949.

Reprints a selection from *Woman in the Nineteenth Century* and "Aspiration" (pp. 367–369).

B 58

The Transcendentalists: An Anthology. Ed. Perry Miller. Cambridge, Mass.: Harvard University Press, 1950.

Reprints selections from the *Memoirs;* "A Short Essay on Critics," "Menzel's View of Goethe," "A Dialogue" (poem), "A Record of Impressions Produced by an Exhibition of Allston's Pictures in the Summer of 1839," and selections from "The Great Lawsuit" from the *Dial* (pp. 332–339, 366–372, 402, 405–407, 457–464).

B 59

American Literature for Colleges. Vol. II, *American Renaissance,* ed. Kinsbury Badger. Harrisburg, Pa.: Stackpole Company, 1954.

Reprints "The Dahlia and the Sun" ("A Dialogue" [poem]), "Descent from the Cross by Raphael," and a selection from "The Great Lawsuit" (pp. 16–24).

B 60
The American Transcendentalists: Their Prose and Poetry. Ed. Perry Miller. Garden City, N.Y.: Doubleday, 1957.

Reprints "A Transcendental Conversation" from the *Memoirs,* "American Literature," "Encouragement," and a selection from *Woman in the Nineteenth Century;* and incorrectly attributes "Dryad Song" to Fuller (pp. 102–103, 189–194, 258–261, 330–339).

B 61
Confessions and Self-Portraits: 4600 Years of Autobiography. Ed. Saul K. Padover. New York: John Day, 1957.

Reprints "Books Change Her Life" from the *Memoirs* (pp. 277–280).

B 62
Love Letters. Ed. John Fostini. New York: Speller & Sons, 1958.

Reprints letter of 25 November 1843 on Beethoven from the *Memoirs* (pp. 79–81).

B 63
Autobiography of Brook Farm. Ed. Henry W. Sams. Englewood Cliffs, N.J.: Prentice-Hall, 1958.

Reprints letter of 28 October 1840 from Thomas Wentworth Higginson, *Margaret Fuller Ossoli* (Boston: Houghton, Mifflin, 1884) (p. 5); of 10 May 1841 to Emerson from Higginson (p. 20); of 16 October 1842 to Emerson from *The Letters of Ralph Waldo Emerson* (1939) (p. 78); and comments on Brook Farm from the *Memoirs* (pp. 215–219).

B 64
Letters to Mother: An Anthology. Ed. Charles Van Doren. Great Neck, N.Y.: Channel Press, 1959.

Reprints letters to her mother of 1 December 1849 and 14 May 1850 from the *Memoirs* (pp. 29–31).

B 65
Thoreau: Man of Concord. Ed. Walter Harding. New York: Holt, Rinehart and Winston, 1960.

Reprints letter of 1841? to Richard Fuller on Thoreau from Margaret Bell, *Margaret Fuller* (New York: Charles Boni, 1930) (p. 153).

B 66
The Educated Woman in America: Selected Writings of Catherine Beecher, Margaret Fuller, and M. Carey Thomas. Ed. Barbara M. Cross. New York: Teachers College Press, 1965.

Reprints selections about "Father," "Schoolteaching," and "Conversations" from the *Memoirs;* letters of 29 September 1840 to Emerson, 26 December 1844 to Elizabeth Peabody, 11 December 1849 to Ellen Fuller Channing, 30 December 1849 to Caroline Sturgis, and 8 January 1850 to Richard Fuller (pp. 105–136).

B 67
The Recognition of Edgar Allan Poe. Ed. Eric W. Carlson. Ann Arbor: University of Michigan Press, 1966.

Reprints "Poe's Tales" from the 11 July 1845 *Tribune* (pp. 17–18).

B 68
Selected Writings of the American Transcendentalists. Ed. George Hochfield. New York: New American Library, 1966.

Reprints "A Short Essay on Critics," "A Dialogue. Poet. Critic." and "The Great Lawsuit" (pp. 297–303, 328–330, 357–367); and incorrectly assigns Fuller partial authorship of "The Editors to the Readers" from the *Dial*.

B 69
Reality and Myth in American Literature. Ed. Kay S. House. Greenwich, Conn.: Fawcett Publications, 1966.

Reprints a selection from "American Literature" (pp. 154–155).

B 70
The Recognition of Herman Melville. Ed. Hershel Parker. Ann Arbor: University of Michigan Press, 1967.

Reprints "Review of *Typee*" from the 4 April 1846 *Tribune* (p. 3).

B 71
Prairie State: Impressions of Illinois, 1673–1967, By Travelers and Other Observers. Ed. Paul M. Angle and Mary Lynn McCree. Chicago: University of Chicago Press, 1968.

Reprints "The Fox River Valley and the Rock River Country" from *Summer on the Lakes* (pp. 213–225).

B 72
The Annals of America. Vol. VII. Publ. William Benton. Chicago: Encyclopedia Britannica, 1968.

Reprints "On the Emancipation of Woman" from *Woman in the Nineteenth Century* (pp. 296–299).

B 73
Up from the Pedestal: Selected Writings in the History of American Feminism. Ed. Aileen S. Kraditor. Chicago: Quadrangle Books, 1968.

Reprints selections from "The Great Lawsuit" (pp. 67–70).

B 74
Readings in American Criticism. Ed. Thomas Elliott Berry. N.p.: Odyssey Press, 1970.

Reprints "A Short Essay on Critics," and "Three Classes of Literature" from the 4 March 1845 *Tribune* (pp. 67–75).

B 75
The Recognition of Ralph Waldo Emerson. Ed. Milton R. Konvitz. Ann Arbor: University of Michigan Press, 1972.

Reprints "Emerson's *Essays*" from the 7 December 1844 *Tribune* (pp. 20–25).

B 76
The American Sisterhood: Writings of the Feminist Movement from Colonial Time to the Present. Ed. Wendy Martin. New York: Harper & Row, 1972.

Reprints a selection from *Woman in the Nineteenth Century* (pp. 205–207).

B 77
The Native Muse: Theories of American Literature. Ed. Richard Ruland. New York: E. P. Dutton, 1972.

Reprints selections from the *Dial* and from "American Literature" (pp. 340–344).

B 78
Feminism: The Essential Historical Writings. Ed. Miriam Schneir. New York: Vintage Books, 1972.

Reprints a selection from *Woman in the Nineteenth Century* (pp. 63–71).

B 79
The Feminist Papers: From Adams to de Beauvoir. Ed. Alice S. Rossi. New York: Columbia University Press, 1973.

Reprints selections from "The Great Lawsuit" (pp. 158–182).

B 80
The Perfectionists: Radical Social Thought in the North, 1815–1860. Ed. Laurence Veysey. New York: John Wiley, 1973.

Reprints as "Womanhood and Individuality" selections from "The Great Lawsuit" (pp. 157–174).

B 81
Sex and Equality. New York: Arno Press, 1974.

Reprints "The Great Lawsuit."

B 82
The Roots of American Feminist Thought. Ed. James L. Cooper and Sheila McIsaac Cooper. Boston: Allyn and Bacon, 1974.

Reprints *Woman in the Nineteenth Century* (pp. 107–130).

B 83
White on Red: Images of the American Indian. Ed. Nancy B. Black and Bette S. Weidman. Port Washington, N.Y.: Kennikat, 1976.

Reprints selections from *Summer on the Lakes* (pp. 210–213).

C. Writings in Newspapers, Magazines, and Journals

C 1

"In Defense of Brutus." *Boston Daily Advertiser & Patriot,* 27 November 1834, p. 2.

Signed "J."

C 2

Review of George Crabbe, *The Life of the Rev. George Crabbe,* and William Roberts, *Memoirs of the Life and Correspondence of Mrs. Hannah More. Western Messenger,* 1 (June 1835), 20–29.

Signed "S.M.F." in the table of contents.

C 3

"The Pilgrims of the Rhine." *Western Messenger,* 1 (August 1835), 101–108.

Review of E. Bulwer-Lytton, *The Last Days of Pompeii.*

C 4

"Philip Van Artevelde." *Western Messenger,* 1 (December 1835), 398–408.

Review of Henry Taylor, *Philip Van Artevelde.* Reprinted: *Life Without and Life Within,* pp. 127–140; as "Classical and Romantic," *Margaret Fuller: American Romantic,* pp. 36–46.

C 5

"Thoughts on Sunday Morning when Prevented by a Snow-storm from Going to Church." *Western Messenger,* 1 (January 1836), 489–490.

Reprinted: *Life Without and Life Within,* pp. 371–373.

C 6

"Lines . . . On the Death of C.C.E." *Boston Daily Centinel & Gazette,* 17 May 1836, p. 1.

Signed "F." Kenneth Walter Cameron, "Margaret Fuller's Poem on the Death of Charles Chauncy Emerson," *Emerson Society Quarterly,* no. 18 (I Quarter 1960), pp. 49–50, first attributed this poem to Fuller; her undated letter to Richard Fuller (MH) makes her authorship definite.

C 7

"Modern British Poets." *American Monthly Magazine,* n.s. 2 (September 1836), 235–250.

Signed "M.F."; concluded in the October number.

C 8

"Modern British Poets." *American Monthly Magazine,* n.s. 2 (October 1836), 320–333.

Signed "M.F." Reprinted: *Papers on Literature and Art*, I, 58–99; *Art, Literature, and the Drama*, pp. 68–109; *The Writings of Margaret Fuller*, pp. 312–346.

C 9
"Jesus, the Comforter." *Western Messenger*, 4 (September 1837), 20–21.

Reprinted: as "Lines Written in March, 1836," *Woman in the Nineteenth Century, and Kindred Papers*, pp. 353–356.

C 10
"Karl Theodor Korner." *Western Messenger*, 4 (January 1838), 306–311.

Signed "S.M.F."; concluded in the February number.

C 11
"Karl Theodor Korner." *Western Messenger*, 4 (February 1838), 369–375.

Signed "S.M.F."

C 12
"Letters from Palmyra." *Western Messenger*, 5 (April 1838), 24–29.

Signed "S.M.F." Review of William Ware, *Letters from Palmyra*.

C 13
"Chat in Boston Bookstores.—No. I." *Boston Quarterly Review*, 3 (January 1840), 127–134.

C 14
Dahlia. "Chat in Boston Bookstores.—No. II." *Boston Quarterly Review*, 3 (July 1840), 323–331.

Dahlia is a pseudonym used by Fuller.

C 15
"A Short Essay on Critics." *Dial*, 1 (July 1840), 5–11.

Signed "F." Reprinted: *Papers on Literature and Art*, I, 1–8; *Art, Literature, and the Drama*, pp. 13–20; *The Writings of Margaret Fuller*, pp. 223–229; *Margaret Fuller: American Romantic*, pp. 66–74; *Margaret Fuller: Essays*, pp. 51–57.

C 16
"A Record of Impressions produced by the Exhibition of Mr. Allston's Pictures in the summer of 1839." *Dial*, 1 (July 1840), 73–83.

Reprinted: *Papers on Literature and Art*, II, 108–120; *Art, Literature, and the Drama*, pp. 284–297.

C 17
"A Dialogue." *Dial*, 1 (July 1840), 134.

C 18
"Richter." *Dial*, 1 (July 1840), 135.

Reprinted: *Life Without and Life Within*, pp. 383–384.

C 19

"Some murmur at the 'want of system' in Richter's Writings." Dial, 1 (July 1840), 135.

Reprinted: as "Richter," *Life Without and Life Within*, pp. 383–384.

C 20

"The Morning Breeze." *Dial*, 1 (July 1840), 135.

C 21

"The Atheneum Exhibition of Painting and Sculpture." *Dial*, 1 (October 1840), 260–263.

C 22

"Meta." *Dial*, 1 (January 1841), 293–298.

Dated "1833". Reprinted: as "Klopstock and Meta," *Life Without and Life Within*, pp. 308–313.

C 23

"The Magnolia of Lake Pontchartrain." *Dial*, 1 (January 1841), 299–305.

Reprinted: *Life Without and Life Within*, pp. 330–336.

C 24

"Menzel's View of Goethe." *Dial*, 1 (January 1841), 340–347.

Signed "F." Reprinted: *Life Without and Life Within*, pp. 13–22.

C 25

Review of B. Rodman, *A Voice from the Prison. Dial*, 1 (January 1841), 404–405.

C 26

Review of N. Hawthorne, *Grandfather's Chair. Dial*, 1 (January 1841), 405.

Reprinted: as "Hawthorne's *Grandfather's Chair*," *Margaret Fuller: Essays*, p. 58.

C 27

"Leila." *Dial*, 1 (April 1841), 462–467.

C 28

"A Dialogue. Poet. Critic." *Dial*, 1 (April 1841), 494–496.

Signed "F." Reprinted: *Papers on Literature and Art*, I, 11–14; *Art, Literature, and the Drama*, pp. 21–24.

C 29

"Goethe." *Dial*, 2 (July 1841), 1–41.

Signed "F." Reprinted: *Life Without and Life Within*, pp. 23–60; *The Writings of Margaret Fuller*, pp. 242–272; *Margaret Fuller: American Romantic*, pp. 77–107.

C 30

Review of T. Carlyle, *On Heroes, Hero-Worship, and the Heroic in History. Dial*, 2 (July 1841), 131–133.

C 31
Review of J. R. Lowell, *A Year's Life. Dial*, 2 (July 1841), 133–134.

Reprinted: as "Lowell's *A Year's Life*," *Margaret Fuller: Essays*, p. 59.

C 32
Review of *Faust*, trans. Abraham Heyward, and Goethe, *Correspondence with a Child. Dial*, 2 (July 1841), 134.

C 33
Review of H. Martineau, *The Hour and the Man. Dial*, 2 (July 1841), 134–135.

C 34
"Tennyson's Poems.—Stirling's Poems.—Festus." Dial, 2 (July 1841), 135.

C 35
Review of the *Plain Speaker* of Providence. *Dial*, 2 (July 1841), 135–136.

C 36
"To Contributors." *Dial*, 2 (July 1841), 136.

C 37
"Literature and Life." *New-Yorker*, 11 (3 July 1841), 246.

Reprinted from "Goethe."

C 38
"Goethe." *New-Yorker*, 11 (10 July 1841), 264.

Reprinted from "Goethe."

C 39
"Goethe." *New-York Daily Tribune*, 16 July 1841, p. 4.

Reprinted from "Goethe" from the *New-Yorker*.

C 40
"Lives of the Great Composers, Haydn, Mozart, Handel, Bach, Beethoven." *Dial*, 2 (October 1841), 148–203.

Signed "F." Reprinted: *Papers on Literature and Art*, II, 46–107; *Art, Literature, and the Drama*, pp. 222–283.

C 41
"Instrumental Music." *Dial*, 2 (October 1841), 172.

Reprinted (with article on composers): *Papers on Literature and Art*, II, 72–73; *Art, Literature, and the Drama*, pp. 249–250.

C 42
"Beethoven." *Dial*, 2 (October 1841), 173.

Reprinted (with article on composers): *Papers on Literature and Art*, II, 73; *Art, Literature, and the Drama*, p. 250.

C 43
"Mozart." *Dial*, 2 (October 1841), 173.

Reprinted (with article on composers): *Papers on Literature and Art*, II, 73; *Art, Literature, and the Drama*, p. 250.

C 44

"Festus." *Dial*, 2 (October 1841), 231–261.

Signed "F." Review of Philip James Bailey, *Festus; a Poem.*

C 45

"Literature and Life." *New-York Mirror*, 19 (9 October 1841), 323.

Reprinted from "Goethe," probably from the 3 July *New-Yorker.*

C 46

"Yuca Filamentosa." *Dial*, 2 (January 1842), 286–288.

C 47

"Bettine Brentano and Her Friend Günderode." *Dial*, 2 (January 1842), 313–357.

Signed "F." Reprinted in part as "Preface," *Günderode* (A 3), pp. viii–xii.

C 48

"Epilogue to the Tragedy of Essex." *Dial*, 2 (January 1842), 380–382.

Translated from Goethe. Reprinted: *Life Without and Life Within*, pp. 400–403.

C 49

Review of Goethe, *Egmont. Dial*, 2 (January 1842), 394–395.

C 50

Review of Washington Allston, *Monaldi, a Tale. Dial*, 2 (January 1842), 395–399.

C 51

Review of Richard H. Wilde, *Conjectures and Researches concerning the Love, Madness, and Imprisonment of Torquato Tasso. Dial*, 2 (January 1842), 399–407.

C 52

"Boston Academy of Music." *Dial*, 2 (January 1842), 407–408.

C 53

Review of *Theory of Teaching. Dial*, 2 (January 1842), 408.

C 54

"Entertainments of the Past Winter." *Dial*, 3 (July 1842), 46–72.

C 55

Review of N. Hawthorne, *Twice-Told Tales. Dial*, 3 (July 1842), 130–131.

Reprinted: as "Hawthorne's *Twice-Told Tales*," *Margaret Fuller: Essays*, pp. 60–61.

C 56

Review of N. Hawthorne, *Biographical Stories for Children. Dial*, 3 (July 1842), 131.

C 57

"Romaic and Rhine Ballads." *Dial*, 3 (October 1842), 137–180.

C 58
Review of A. Tennyson, *Poems. Dial,* 3 (October 1842), 273–276.

C 59
"Canova." *Dial,* 3 (April 1843), 454–483.

C 60
Review of Francis J. Festis, *Music Explained. Dial,* 3 (April 1843), 533–534.

C 61
"The Great Lawsuit. Man *versus* Men. Woman *versus* Women." *Dial,* 4 (July 1843), 1–47.

Revised and expanded as *Woman in the Nineteenth Century* (A 5).

C 62
"Woman—Her Sphere and Education." *New-York Daily Tribune,* 17 July 1843, p. 4.

Reprinted from "The Great Lawsuit."

C 63
"Woman—Her Sphere and Needs." *New-York Weekly Tribune,* 22 July 1843, p. 1.

Reprinted from "The Great Lawsuit."

C 64
"Woman—Her Sphere and Education." *New-York Weekly Tribune,* 22 July 1843, p. 2.

Reprinted from "The Great Lawsuit" from the *Daily Tribune.*

C 65
"The Modern Drama." *Dial,* 4 (January 1844), 307–349.

Review of J. Westland Marston, *The Patrician's Daughter;* William H. Smith, *Athelwold;* and J. Sterling, *Strafford.* Reprinted: *Papers on Literature and Art,* I, 100–150; *Art, Literature, and the Drama,* pp. 110–160.

C 66
Review of L. M. Child, *Letters from New York. Dial,* 4 (January 1844), 407.

C 67
"The Two Herberts." *Present,* 1 (1 March 1844), 301–312.

Signed "S.M. Fuller." Reprinted: *Papers on Literature and Art,* I, 15–34; *Art, Literature, and the Drama,* pp. 25–44; *The Writings of Margaret Fuller,* pp. 273–289.

C 68
"Dialogue." *Dial,* 4 (April 1844), 458–469.

Reprinted: *Papers on Literature and Art,* I, 151–164; *Art, Literature, and the Drama,* pp. 161–174.

C 69
"Life on the Prairies." *New-York Weekly Tribune,* 15 June 1844, p. 1.

Reprinted from *Summer on the Lakes.*

C 70

"On Woman." *The New Age, Concordium Gazette, and Temperance Advocate* (England), 1 (1 November 1844), 305–308.

Reprinted from "The Great Lawsuit."

C 71

"Emerson's Essays." *New-York Daily Tribune*, 7 December 1844, p. 1:1–3.

Review of R. W. Emerson, *Essays: Second Series.* Reprinted: *New-York Weekly Tribune*, 14 December 1844, p. 2; *Life Without and Life Within*, pp. 191–198; *The Writings of Margaret Fuller*, pp. 389–395; *Margaret Fuller: American Romantic*, pp. 191–200; *Margaret Fuller: Essays*, pp. 240–247.

C 72

"Mr. Hosmer's Poems." *New-York Daily Tribune*, 11 December 1844, p. 1:1–2.

Review of William H. C. Hosmer, *Yonnodio.* Reprinted: *New-York Weekly Tribune*, 21 December 1844, p. 2.

C 73

"Cranch's Poems." *New-York Daily Tribune*, 12 December 1844, p. 1:1.

Review of C. P. Cranch, *Poems.* Reprinted: *New-York Weekly Tribune*, 21 December 1844, p. 2.

C 74

"Thanksgiving." *New-York Daily Tribune*, 12 December 1844, p. 2:1–2.

Reprinted: *New-York Weekly Tribune*, 14 December 1844, p. 1; *Life Without and Life Within*, pp. 243–249; *Margaret Fuller: Essays*, pp. 248–253.

C 75

"Monument to Goethe." *New-York Daily Tribune*, 16 December 1844, p. 1:2.

From the *Deutsche Schnellpost.* Reprinted: *New-York Weekly Tribune*, 21 December 1844, p. 2.

C 76

"Ole Bull." *New-York Daily Tribune*, 20 December 1844, p. 2:3.

Reprinted: *New-York Weekly Tribune*, 28 December 1844, p. 6.

C 77

"Christmas." *New-York Weekly Tribune*, 21 December 1844, p. 1:1–3.

Reprinted: *New-York Daily Tribune*, 25 December 1844, p. 1; *Woman in the Nineteenth Century, and Kindred Papers*, pp. 300–309; *Life Without and Life Within*, pp. 250–257; *Margaret Fuller: Essays*, pp. 254–260.

C 78

"New Year's Day." *New-York Weekly Tribune*, 28 December 1844, p. 1:1–3.

Reprinted: *New-York Daily Tribune*, 1 January 1845, p. 1; *Life Without and Life Within*, pp. 219–225; *Margaret Fuller: Essays*, pp. 261–266.

C 79
"Ole Bull." *New-York Daily Tribune*, 30 December 1844, p. 2:3.

C 80
"Miss Barrett's Poems." *New-York Daily Tribune*, 4 January 1845, p. 1:1–4.

Review of E. B. Barrett, *A Drama of Exile and Other Poems*. Reprinted: *New-York Weekly Tribune*, 18 January 1845, p. 2; *Papers on Literature and Art*, II, 22–30; *Art, Literature, and the Drama*, pp. 198–206; *The Woman and the Myth*, pp. 203–205.

C 81
"German Newspapers." *New-York Daily Tribune*, 6 January 1845, p. 2:5.

C 82
"The Liberty Bell for 1845." *New-York Daily Tribune*, 7 January 1845, p. 1:3.

Reprinted: *New-York Weekly Tribune*, 18 January 1845, p. 2.

C 83
"Franz Liszt and Eugene Sue." *New-York Daily Tribune*, 11 January 1845, p. 1:1.

From the *Deutsche Schnellpost*. Reprinted: *New-York Weekly Tribune*, 18 January 1845, p. 1.

C 84
"The North American Review [for January]." *New-York Daily Tribune*, 13 January 1845, p. 1:1–3.

Reprinted: *New-York Weekly Tribune*, 18 January 1845, p. 1.

C 85
"Italian Opera on Friday Night." *New-York Daily Tribune*, 13 January 1845, p. 2:3.

C 86
Review of H. W. Longfellow, *The Waif: A Collection of Poems*. *New-York Daily Tribune*, 16 January 1845, p. 1:1–2.

Reprinted: *New-York Weekly Tribune*, 25 January 1845, p. 2.

C 87
Review of Charles Lanman, *Letters from a Landscape Painter*. *New-York Daily Tribune*, 18 January 1845, p. 1:1.

Reprinted: *New-York Weekly Tribune*, 25 January 1845, p. 2; as "Letters from a Landscape Painter," *Life Without and Life Within*, pp. 69–70.

C 88
"Music in New-York." *New-York Daily Tribune*, 18 January 1845, p. 2:3.

Unsigned. Reprinted: *New-York Weekly Tribune*, 25 January 1845, p. 1..

C 89
Review of J. R. Lowell, *Conversations on Some of the Old Poets*. *New-York Daily Tribune*, 21 January 1845, p. 1:1–3.

Reprinted: *New-York Weekly Tribune*, 25 January 1845, p. 1.

C 90
"Edgar A. Poe." *New-York Daily Tribune,* 24 January 1845, p. 1:1.

Review of the February 1845 *Graham's Magazine.* Reprinted: *New-York Weekly Tribune,* 1 February 1845, p. 2.

C 91
"Deutsche Schnellpost." *New-York Daily Tribune,* 25 January 1845, p. 1:1–2.

Reprinted: *New-York Weekly Tribune,* 1 February 1845, p. 2; *Life Without and Life Within,* pp. 174–178.

C 92
"Popular Literature in Germany. By Gottfried Kinkel." *New-York Daily Tribune,* 27 January 1845, p. 1:1–2.

From the *Deutsche Schnellpost.* Reprinted: *New-York Weekly Tribune,* 1 February 1845, p. 2.

C 93
Review of L. H. Sigourney, *Scenes in My Native Land. New-York Daily Tribune,* 28 January 1845, p. 1:1–3.

Reprinted: *New-York Weekly Tribune,* 1 February 1845, p. 1; as "Americans and Their Love of Nature," *Margaret Fuller: American Romantic,* pp. 200–201.

C 94
"French Novelists of the Day: Balzac . . . . George Sand . . . . Eugene Sue." *New-York Daily Tribune,* 1 February 1845, p. 1:1–4.

Reprinted: *New-York Weekly Tribune,* 22 February 1845, p. 2; as "French Novelists of the Day," *Life Without and Life Within,* pp. 158–168; *The Writings of Margaret Fuller,* pp. 301–311; *The Woman and the Myth,* pp. 205–207.

C 95
Review of *The Slave: or Memoirs of Archy Moore. New-York Daily Tribune,* 4 February 1845, p. 1:1.

C 96
Review of *Revue Francais des Familles,* ed. F. G. Berteau. *New-York Daily Tribune,* 4 February 1845, p. 1:1.

C 97
Review of *The Child's Friend,* ed. Eliza L. Follen. *New-York Daily Tribune,* 5 February 1845, p. 1:1–2.

Reprinted: *New-York Weekly Tribune,* 22 February 1845, p. 1; as "Children's Books," *Woman in the Nineteenth Century, and Kindred Papers,* pp. 310–313; *The Woman and the Myth,* p. 347; *Margaret Fuller: Essays,* pp. 267–270.

C 98
Review of *Life of Beethoven,* ed. Ionace Moscelles. *New-York Daily Tribune,* 7 February 1845, p. 1:1–3.

Reprinted: *New-York Weekly Tribune,* 8 February 1845, p. 1; as "Beethoven," *Life Without and Life Within,* pp. 71–82.

C 99
Review of Henry R. Schoolcraft, *Oneota, or the Red Race of America*. *New-York Daily Tribune*, 12 February 1845, p. 1:1–3.

Reprinted: *New-York Weekly Tribune*, 15 February 1845, p. 1.

C 100
Review of J. Stanley Grimes, *Etherology or the Philosophy of Mesmerism and Phrenology*. *New-York Daily Tribune*, 17 February 1845, p. 1:1–2.

Reprinted: *New-York Weekly Tribune*, 22 February 1845, p. 2; as "The New Science, or the Philosophy of Mesmerism or Animal Magnetism," *Life Without and Life Within*, pp. 169–173; as "Etherology," *Margaret Fuller: Essays*, pp. 271–276.

C 101
"Mr. Hudson's Lecture on Hamlet." *New-York Daily Tribune*, 19 February 1845, p. 2:2.

Reprinted: *New-York Weekly Tribune*, 22 February 1845, p. 1.

C 102
"St. Valentine's Day—Bloomingdale Asylum for the Insane." *New-York Daily Tribune*, 22 February 1845, p. 1:1–2.

Reprinted: *New-York Weekly Tribune*, 1 March 1845, p. 2; as "St. Valentine's Day," *Life Without and Life Within*, pp. 226–231; *Margaret Fuller: Essays*, pp. 277–281.

C 103
"Cheap Postage Bill." *New-York Daily Tribune*, 24 February 1845, p. 2:2.

Reprinted: *New-York Weekly Tribune*, 1 March 1845, p. 6; *Margaret Fuller: Essays*, pp. 282–283.

C 104
"Letters from Warsaw." *New-York Daily Tribune*, 24 February 1845, p. 2:2.

From the *Deutsche Schnellpost*. Reprinted: *New-York Weekly Tribune*, 1 March 1845, p. 6.

C 105
Review of A. Dumas, *The Regent's Daughter*. *New-York Daily Tribune*, 25 February 1845, p. 2:2.

Reprinted: *New-York Weekly Tribune*, 1 March 1845, p. 1.

C 106
Review of T. Parker, *The Excellence of Goodness*. *New-York Daily Tribune*, 26 February 1845, p. 1:1–2.

Reprinted: *New-York Weekly Tribune*, 1 March 1845, p. 1; as "The Excellence of Goodness," *Margaret Fuller: Essays*, pp. 284–288.

C 107
"English Writers Little Known Here. Milnes .... Landor .... Julius Hare." *New-York Daily Tribune*, 4 March 1845, p. 1:1–5.

Reprinted: *New-York Weekly Tribune*, 8 March 1845, p. 1; selection, as "Three Classes of Literature," *The Writings of Margaret Fuller*, pp. 230–231.

C 108
"Music in New-York." *New-York Daily Tribune,* 6 March 1845, p. 2:2.

Reprinted: *New-York Weekly Tribune,* 15 March 1845, p. 6.

C 109
"Concert by the German Society." *New-York Daily Tribune,* 10 March 1845, p. 2:4.

Reprinted: *New-York Weekly Tribune,* 15 March 1845, p. 6.

C 110
"New Year's Letter from the Catholic Priest, Ronge." *New-York Daily Tribune,* 12 March 1845, p. 1:1–2.

From the *Deutsche Schnellpost.* Reprinted: *New-York Weekly Tribune,* 15 March 1845, p. 1.

C 111
Review of J. P. F. Richter, *Flower, Fruit and Thorn Pieces. New-York Daily Tribune,* 12 March 1845, p. 1:2.

Reprinted: *New-York Weekly Tribune,* 15 March 1845, p. 1.

C 112
Review of Ida, Countess Hahn-Hahn, *The Countess Faustina. New-York Daily Tribune,* 12 March 1845, p. 1:2.

Reprinted: *New-York Weekly Tribune,* 15 March 1845, p. 1.

C 113
"Translations from the German." *New-York Daily Tribune,* 14 March 1845, p. 1:1–2.

Review of *Correspondence Between Schiller and Goethe,* trans. George H. Calvert. Reprinted: *New-York Weekly Tribune,* 15 March 1845, p. 1.

C 114
"Our City Charities. Visit to Bellevue Alms House, to the Farm School, the Asylum for the Insane, and Penitentiary on Blackwell's Island." *New-York Daily Tribune,* 19 March 1845, p. 1:1–3.

Reprinted: *New-York Weekly Tribune,* 22 March 1845, p. 1; *The Woman and the Myth,* pp. 337–340.

C 115
"Writers Little Known Among Us. Milnes . . . Landor . . . Julius Hare." *New-York Daily Tribune,* 28 March 1845, p. 1:1–3.

Reprinted: *New-York Weekly Tribune,* 29 March 1845, p. 1.

C 116
Review of T. Parker, *A Letter to the Boston Association of Congregational Ministers,* and W. H. Furness, *The Exclusive Principle Considered. New-York Daily Tribune,* 29 March 1845, p. 1:1.

Reprinted: *New-York Weekly Tribune,* 5 April 1845, p. 2.

C 117
"Frederick Von Raumer upon the Slavery Question." *New-York Daily Tribune*, 29 March 1845, p. 1:2.

Reprinted: *New-York Weekly Tribune*, 5 April 1845, p. 2.

C 118
"Library of Choice Reading." *New-York Daily Tribune*, 4 April 1845, p. 1:1–3.

Review of Friedrich Foque, *Undine and Sintram, The Amber Witch*, and *Eothen*. Reprinted: *New-York Weekly Tribune*, 5 April 1845, p. 1.

C 119
"Palmo's.—The Antigone." *New-York Daily Tribune*, 16 April 1845, p. 2:3.

Reprinted: *New-York Weekly Tribune*, 19 April 1845, p. 4.

C 120
"The Modern Jews." *New-York Daily Tribune*, 21 April 1845, p. 1:1–3.

Review of the April *North American Review*. Reprinted: *New-York Weekly Tribune*, 26 April 1845, p. 1.

C 121
"Philharmonic Concert on Saturday Evening, April 19th." *New-York Daily Tribune*, 22 April 1845, p. 2:2.

Reprinted: *New-York Weekly Tribune*, 26 April 1845, p. 5.

C 122
"Hazlitt's Table-Talk." *New-York Daily Tribune*, 30 April 1845, p. 1:1.

Reprinted: *New-York Weekly Tribune*, 3 May 1845, p. 1.

C 123
"Ertheiler's Phrase-Book." *New-York Daily Tribune*, 1 May 1845, p. 2:3.

Reprinted: *New-York Weekly Tribune*, 10 May 1845, p. 1.

C 124
"Kneeland, the Sculptor." *New-York Daily Tribune*, 3 May 1845, p. 2:2.

C 125
"Com. Wilkes's Narrative." *New-York Daily Tribune*, 7 May 1845, p. 1:2.

Review of Charles Wilkes, *Narrative of the United States Exploring Expedition*. Reprinted: *New-York Weekly Tribune*, 10 May 1845, p. 1.

C 126
"Mrs. Child's Letters." *New-York Daily Tribune*, 10 May 1845, p. 1:1–3.

Review of L. M. Child, *Letters from New York. Second Series*. Reprinted: *New-York Weekly Tribune*, 10 May 1845, p. 1.

C 127
Review of Charles Anthon, *A System of Latin Versification*. *New-York Daily Tribune*, 12 May 1845, p. 1:1.

Reprinted: *New-York Weekly Tribune,* 17 May 1845, p. 5; as "A Transcendental Defense of Classical Metres," *Margaret Fuller: American Romantic,* pp. 205–207.

C 128
Review of *Saul. A Mystery. New-York Daily Tribune,* 12 May 1845, p. 1:1.

Reprinted: *New-York Weekly Tribune,* 17 May 1845, p. 5.

C 129
Review of Thomas Love Peacock, *Headlong Hall* and *Nightmare Abbey. New-York Daily Tribune,* 12 May 1845, p. 1:2.

Reprinted: *New-York Weekly Tribune,* 17 May 1845, p. 5.

C 130
Review of Tatler Lewis, *Plato Against the Atheists. New-York Daily Tribune,* 14 May 1845, p. 1:1.

Reprinted: *New-York Weekly Tribune,* 17 May 1845, p. 1.

C 131
Review of W. W. Lord, *Poems. New-York Daily Tribune,* 19 May 1845, p. 1:1.

Reprinted: *New-York Weekly Tribune,* 31 May 1845, p. 1.

C 132
" 'American Facts.' " *New-York Daily Tribune,* 19 May 1845, p. 1:1.

Review of George P. Putnam, *American Facts.* Reprinted: *New-York Weekly Tribune,* 24 May 1845, p. 1; *Life Without and Life Within,* pp. 108–109; *Margaret Fuller: American Romantic,* pp. 207–209; *Margaret Fuller: Essays,* pp. 289–290.

C 133
"Michelet's History of France." *New-York Daily Tribune,* 20 May 1845, p. 1:1–2.

Reprinted: *New-York Weekly Tribune,* 31 May 1845, p. 6.

C 134
Review of *The French in Algiers. New-York Daily Tribune,* 22 May 1845, p. 1:1.

Reprinted: *New-York Weekly Tribune,* 31 May 1845, p. 6.

C 135
Review of Goethe, *Essays on Art,* trans. S. G. Ward. *New-York Daily Tribune,* 29 May 1845, p. 1:1.

Reprinted: *New-York Weekly Tribune,* 7 June 1845, p. 6.

C 136
Review of *Select Tales from Gesta Romanorum. New-York Daily Tribune,* 31 May 1845, p. 1:1–3.

Reprinted: *New-York Weekly Tribune,* 7 June 1845, p. 1.

C 137
"Prevalent Idea that Politeness is too Great a Luxury to be given to the Poor." *New-York Daily Tribune,* 31 May 1845, p. 2:2.

Reprinted: *New-York Weekly Tribune*, 7 June 1845, p. 3; as "Politeness Too Great a Luxury to be Given to the Poor," *Life Without and Life Within*, pp. 322–325; *Margaret Fuller: Essays*, pp. 291–293.

C 138
Review of L. M. Child, *Philothea*. *New-York Daily Tribune*, 5 June 1845, p. 1:1.

Reprinted: *New-York Weekly Tribune*, 14 June 1845, p. 6.

C 139
"Courrier des Etats-Unis." *New-York Daily Tribune*, 7 June 1845, p. 1:1.

Reprinted: *New-York Weekly Tribune*, 14 June 1845, p. 6; *Woman in the Nineteenth Century, and Kindred Papers*, pp. 276–279.

C 140
Review of *The Crescent and the Cross*. *New-York Daily Tribune*, 7 June 1845, p. 1:1.

Reprinted: *New-York Weekly Tribune*, 14 June 1845, p. 6.

C 141
Review of *Narrative of the Life of Frederick Douglass, an American Slave*. *New-York Daily Tribune*, 10 June 1845, p. 1:1–2.

Reprinted: *New-York Weekly Tribune*, 14 June 1845, p. 1; as "Frederick Douglass," *Life Without and Life Within*, pp. 121–126; *The Woman and The Myth*, pp. 340–342; *Margaret Fuller: Essays*, pp. 294–296.

C 142
Review of H. W. Longfellow, *The Poets and Poetry of Europe*. *New-York Daily Tribune*, 17 June 1845, p. 1:1–2.

Reprinted: *New-York Weekly Tribune*, 21 June 1845, p. 1.

C 143
"Asylum for Discharged Female Convicts." *New-York Daily Tribune*, 19 June 1845, p. 1:1–2.

Reprinted: *New-York Weekly Tribune*, 28 June 1845, p. 6; as "Appeal for an Asylum for Discharged Female Convicts," *Life Without and Life Within*, pp. 283–286.

C 144
"Story Books for Hot Weather." *New-York Daily Tribune*, 20 June 1845, p. 1:1–2.

Review of Benjamin Disraeli's writings and Nathaniel P. Willis, *Dashes at Life*. Reprinted: *New-York Weekly Tribune*, 28 June 1845, p. 6; *Life Without and Life Within*, pp. 143–148.

C 145
"The Water Cure." *New-York Weekly Tribune*, 21 June 1845, p. 2:1.

Reprinted: *New-York Daily Tribune*, 27 June 1845, p. 1.

C 146
Review of Charles C. Green, *The Nubian Slave*. *New-York Daily Tribune*, 24 June 1845, p. 1:1.

Reprinted: *New-York Weekly Tribune*, 28 June 1845, p. 1.

C 147
"Swedenborgianism." *New-York Daily Tribune*, 25 June 1845, p. 1:1–2.

Review of *Noble's Appeal in Behalf of the Views held by the New Church;* Theophilus Parsons, *Essays;* and R. F. Barrett, *The Corner Stone of the New Jerusalem.* Reprinted: *New-York Weekly Tribune*, 28 June 1845, p. 1; *Papers on Literature and Art*, II, 160–165; *Art, Literature, and the Drama*, pp. 336–341.

C 148
"United States Exploring Expedition." *New-York Daily Tribune*, 28 June 1845, p. 1:1.

Review of Charles Wilkes, *Narrative of the United States Exploring Expedition.* Reprinted: *New-York Weekly Tribune*, 5 July 1845, p. 6; *Life Without and Life Within*, pp. 141–142; *The Woman and the Myth*, pp. 343–344.

C 149
Review of C. Sealsfield, *Tokeah, or the White Rose. New-York Daily Tribune*, 28 June 1845, p. 1:2–3.

Reprinted: *New-York Weekly Tribune*, 5 July 1845, p. 6.

C 150
"The Irish Character." *New-York Daily Tribune*, 28 June 1845, p. 2:2.

Reprinted: *New-York Weekly Tribune*, 5 July 1845, p. 1; *Woman in the Nineteenth Century, and Kindred Papers*, pp. 320–324; *The Woman and the Myth*, pp. 344–346.

C 151
"Glumdalclitches." *New-York Daily Tribune*, 30 June 1845, p. 1:1.

Reprinted: *New-York Weekly Tribune*, 5 July 1845, p. 6; *Woman in the Nineteenth Century, and Kindred Papers*, pp. 266–268.

C 152
Review of John Wilson, *Trials of Margaret Lyndsay* and Alexander Wilson, *The Foresters. New-York Daily Tribune*, 3 July 1845, p. 1:1.

Reprinted: *New-York Weekly Tribune*, 12 July 1845, p. 6.

C 153
"Fourth of July." *New-York Daily Tribune*, 4 July 1845, p. 2:1.

Reprinted: *New-York Weekly Tribune*, 5 July 1845, p. 1; *Life Without and Life Within*, pp. 232–235; as "Fourth of July, 1845," *Margaret Fuller: American Romantic*, pp. 210–213; *Margaret Fuller: Essays*, pp. 297–300.

C 154
"Swedenborg and his Disciples." *New-York Daily Tribune*, 7 July 1845, p. 1:1.

Reprinted: *New-York Weekly Tribune*, 12 July 1845, p. 6.

C 155
Review of Anna C. Mowatt, *Evelyn. New-York Daily Tribune*, 7 July 1845, p. 1:1.

Reprinted: *New-York Weekly Tribune*, 12 July 1845, p. 6.

C 156

"French Gayety." *New-York Daily Tribune,* 9 July 1845, p. 1:1–2.

Reprinted: *New-York Weekly Tribune,* 12 July 1845, p. 1.

C 157

Review of Leigh Hunt, *The Indicator. New-York Daily Tribune,* 11 July 1845, p. 1:1.

Reprinted: *New-York Weekly Tribune,* 12 July 1845, p. 1.

C 158

Review E. A. Poe, *Tales. New-York Daily Tribune,* 11 July 1845, p. 1:2.

Reprinted: *New-York Weekly Tribune,* 19 July 1845, p. 6; as "Poe's Tales," *The Writings of Margaret Fuller,* pp. 396–397; *Margaret Fuller: American Romantic,* pp. 214–215; *Margaret Fuller: Essays,* pp. 301–302.

C 159

"The 'Kosmos' of Alexan. von Humboldt." *New-York Daily Tribune,* 11 July 1845, p. 1:2.

Reprinted: *New-York Weekly Tribune,* 12 July 1845, p. 1.

C 160

"The Irish Character." *New-York Daily Tribune,* 15 July 1845, p. 1:1–2.

Reprinted: *New-York Weekly Tribune,* 19 July 1845, p. 1; *Woman in the Nineteenth Century, and Kindred Papers,* pp. 325–334.

C 161

"Thomas Hood." *New-York Daily Tribune,* 18 July 1845, p. 1:1–3.

Reprinted: *New-York Weekly Tribune,* 19 July 1845, p. 1; *Life Without and Life Within,* pp. 61–68.

C 162

Review of Heinrich Zschokke, *Tales,* ed. P. Godwin. *New-York Daily Tribune,* 22 July 1845, p. 1:1.

Reprinted: *New-York Weekly Tribune,* 26 July 1845, p. 1.

C 163

"Clairvoyance." *New-York Daily Tribune,* 23 July 1845, p. 1:1–2.

Review of Justinus Kerner, *The Seeress of Prevorst* and Gibson Smith, *Lectures on Clairmativeness.* Reprinted: *New-York Weekly Tribune,* 26 July 1845, p. 1.

C 164

"The Irish Character." *New-York Daily Tribune,* 24 July 1845, p. 1:1.

C 165

"Liberation of Dr. Steiger—Indian Funeral in Paris." *New-York Daily Tribune,* 25 July 1845, p. 1:1–2.

From the *Courrier des Etats-Unis.* Reprinted: *New-York Weekly Tribune,* 2 August 1845, p. 2.

C 166
Review of Caroline Norton, *The Child of the Islands* and John Critchley Prince, *Hours with the Muses*. *New-York Daily Tribune*, 26 July 1845, p. 1:1–3.

Reprinted: *New-York Weekly Tribune*, 2 August 1845, p. 1; in "Poets of the People," *Papers on Literature and Art*, II, 14–21; *Art, Literature, and the Drama*, pp. 190–197.

C 167
Review of *Natalia and Other Tales*. *New-York Daily Tribune*, 26 July 1845, p. 2:2.

Reprinted: *New-York Weekly Tribune*, 2 August 1845, p. 6.

C 168
"First of August, 1845." *New-York Daily Tribune*, 1 August 1845, p. 1:1–2.

Reprinted: *New-York Weekly Tribune*, 2 August 1845, p. 1; as "First of August," *Life Without and Life Within*, pp. 236–242.

C 169
"Some Items of Foreign Gossip." *New-York Daily Tribune*, 2 August 1845, p. 1:1.

Reprinted: *New-York Weekly Tribune*, 16 August 1845, p. 6.

C 170
"Courrier des Etats-Unis—Our 'Protegee,' Queen Victoria." *New-York Daily Tribune*, 4 August 1845, p. 1:1–2.

Unsigned. Reprinted: *New-York Weekly Tribune*, 9 August 1845, p. 1; *Woman in the Nineteenth Century, and Kindred Papers*, pp. 280–285.

C 171
"The Social Movement in Europe." *New-York Daily Tribune*, 5 August 1845, p. 1:1–4.

From the *Deutsche Schnellpost*. Reprinted: *New-York Weekly Tribune*, 16 August 1845, p. 6.

C 172
"Thomas Hood." *New-York Daily Tribune*, 9 August 1845, p. 1:1–2.

Review of T. Hood, *Prose and Verse*. Reprinted: *New-York Weekly Tribune*, 9 August 1845, p. 1.

C 173
"Prince's Poems." *New-York Daily Tribune*, 13 August 1845, p. 1:1–3.

Reprinted: *New-York Weekly Tribune*, 16 August 1845, p. 1; in "Poets of the People," *Papers on Literature and Art*, II, 10–14; *Art, Literature, and the Drama*, pp. 186–190.

C 174
Review of Martin F. Tupper, *The Crock of Gold*. *New-York Daily Tribune*, 15 August 1845, p. 1:1–2.

Reprinted: *New-York Weekly Tribune*, 23 August 1845, p. 6.

C 175
"Thom's Poems." *New-York Daily Tribune*, 22 August 1845, p. 1:1–3.

Review of William Thom, *Rhymes and Recollections of a Hand-Loom Weaver*. Reprinted: *New-York Weekly Tribune*, 23 August 1845, p. 1; in "Poets of the People,"

Papers on Literature and Art, II, 1–9; *Art, Literature, and the Drama,* pp. 177–185; as "The Philosophy of Criticism," *Margaret Fuller: American Romantic,* pp. 215–218.

C 176
"School of the Misses Sedgwick." *New-York Daily Tribune,* 25 August 1845, p. 1:1.

C 177
"Items of Foreign Gossip," *New-York Daily Tribune,* 27 August 1845, p. 1:1–2.

Reprinted: *New-York Weekly Tribune,* 30 August 1845, p. 1.

C 178
Review of Thomas Arnold, *Introductory Lectures on Modern History. New-York Daily Tribune,* 28 August 1845, p. 1:1.

Reprinted: *New-York Weekly Tribune,* 30 August 1845, p. 1.

C 179
"The Great Britain." *New-York Daily Tribune,* 30 August 1845, p. 1:1.

Reprinted: *New-York Weekly Tribune,* 30 August 1845, p. 1.

C 180
Review of Sylvester Judd, *Margaret: A Tale of the Real and Ideal, Blight and Bloom. New-York Daily Tribune,* 1 September 1845, p. 1:1.

Reprinted: *New-York Weekly Tribune,* 6 September 1845, p. 1.

C 181
"Who wants to Buy French Embroidery, Novels, Gloves or Claret?" *New-York Daily Tribune,* 1 September 1845, p. 1:1.

C 182
"Frisian Ballad." *New-York Daily Tribune,* 1 September 1845, p. 4:1.

Reprinted: *New-York Weekly Tribune,* 6 September 1845, p. 1.

C 183
"The Beethoven Movement." *New-York Daily Tribune,* 3 September 1845, p. 1:1–2.

Reprinted: *New-York Weekly Tribune,* 6 September 1845, p. 1.

C 184
Review of E. Sue, *The Hotel Lambert. New-York Daily Tribune,* 3 September 1845, p. 1:2.

Reprinted: *New-York Weekly Tribune,* 6 September 1845, p. 1.

C 185
Review of Philip J. Bailey, *Festus. New-York Daily Tribune,* 8 September 1845, p. 1:1–3.

Reprinted: *New-York Weekly Tribune,* 13 September 1845, p. 1; as "Festus," *Life Without and Life Within,* pp. 153–157.

C 186
Review of *The White Slave. New-York Daily Tribune,* 10 September 1845, p. 1:1.

Reprinted: *New-York Weekly Tribune,* 13 September 1845, p. 1.

C 187
Review of C. Lamb, *Essays of Elia*. *New-York Daily Tribune*, 10 September 1845, p. 1:3.

Reprinted: *New-York Weekly Tribune*, 13 September 1845, p. 1.

C 188
Review of *Studies in Religion*. *New-York Daily Tribune*, 11 September 1845, p. 1:1.

Reprinted: *New-York Weekly Tribune*, 20 September 1845, p. 6.

C 189
"The Tailor." *New-York Daily Tribune*, 17 September 1845, p. 1:1–2.

Reprinted: *New-York Weekly Tribune*, 20 September 1845, p. 1.

C 190
"Jenny Lind . . . The Consuelo of George Sand." *New-York Daily Tribune*, 19 September 1845, p. 2:1–2.

Reprinted: *New-York Weekly Tribune*, 27 September 1845, p. 1; *Woman in the Nineteenth Century, and Kindred Papers*, pp. 241–249.

C 191
"Items of Foreign Gossip." *New-York Daily Tribune*, 24 September 1845, p. 1:1–2.

Reprinted: *New-York Weekly Tribune*, 27 September 1845, p. 6.

C 192
"The Wrongs of American Women. The Duty of American Women." *New-York Daily Tribune*, 30 September 1845, p. 1:1–3.

Review of Charles Burdett, *The Wrongs of American Women* and [Catharine Beecher], *The Duty of American Women to Their Country*. Reprinted: *New-York Weekly Tribune*, 4 October 1845, p. 1; *Woman in the Nineteenth Century, and Kindred Papers*, pp. 217–227; *Margaret Fuller: Essays*, pp. 303–310.

C 193
"Ole Bull." *New-York Daily Tribune*, 1 October 1845, p. 1:1–2.

Reprinted: *New-York Weekly Tribune*, 4 October 1845, p. 1.

C 194
Review of *The Prose Works of Milton*, intro. R. W. Griswold. *New-York Daily Tribune*, 7 October 1845, p. 1:1–2.

Reprinted: *New-York Weekly Tribune*, 11 October 1845, p. 1; as "The Prose Works of Milton," *Papers on Literature and Art*, I, 35–42; *Art, Literature, and the Drama*, pp. 45–52.

C 195
Circular about *The Kosmian*, an antislavery publication. *New-York Daily Tribune*, 9 October 1845, supplement, p. 1:4.

C 196
Review of W. G. Simms, *The Wigwam and the Cabin* and Cornelius Mathews, *Big Abel and the Little Manhattan*. *New-York Daily Tribune*, 11 October 1845, p. 1:1.

Reprinted: *New-York Weekly Tribune*, 18 October 1845, p. 1.

C 197

"Italy." *New-York Daily Tribune,* 13 November 1845, p. 1:1–3.

Review of *The Auto-biography of Alfieri, Memoirs of Benvenuto Cellini,* and *Cary's Dante.* Reprinted: *New-York Weekly Tribune,* 15 November 1845, p. 1; as "Alfieri and Cellini," *Life Without and Life Within,* pp. 93–101; as "Italy," *The Writings of Margaret Fuller,* pp. 347–353.

C 198

"The Celestial Empire." *New-York Daily Tribune,* 13 November 1845, p. 2:3.

Reprinted: *New-York Weekly Tribune,* 22 November 1845, p. 6; *Life Without and Life Within,* pp. 304–307.

C 199

"Leopold de Meyer." *New-York Daily Tribune,* 17 November 1845, p. 1:1.

Reprinted: *New-York Weekly Tribune,* 22 November 1845, p. 1.

C 200

"Italy." *New-York Daily Tribune,* 18 November 1845, p. 1:2–3.

Review of *Cary's Dante* and *The Lyrical Poems of Dante,* trans. Charles Lyell. Reprinted: *New-York Weekly Tribune,* 22 November 1845, p. 1; as "Italy.—Cary's Dante," *Life Without and Life Within,* pp. 102–107; *The Writings of Margaret Fuller,* pp. 353–357.

C 201

Review of L. M. Child, *History of Women. New-York Daily Tribune,* 20 November 1845, p. 1:1.

Reprinted: *New-York Weekly Tribune,* 29 November 1845, p. 6.

C 202

Review of George W. Burnap, *Miscellaneous Writings. New-York Weekly Tribune,* 20 November 1845, p. 6:3.

Reprinted: *New-York Daily Tribune,* 21 November 1845, p. 1.

C 203

Review of Caroline M. Kirkland, *Western Clearings. New-York Daily Tribune,* 21 November 1845, p. 1:1–2.

Reprinted: *New-York Weekly Tribune,* 29 November 1845, p. 6.

C 204

Review of E. A. Poe, *The Raven and Other Poems. New-York Daily Tribune,* 26 November 1845, p. 1:4–5.

Reprinted: *New-York Weekly Tribune,* 29 November 1845, p. 1; as "Edgar A. Poe," *Life Without and Life Within,* pp. 87–92; as "Poe's Poems," *The Writings of Margaret Fuller,* pp. 398–403; as "Poe's *The Raven and Other Poems,*" *Margaret Fuller: Essays,* pp. 311–316.

C 205

Review of V. Hugo, *The Rhine. New-York Daily Tribune,* 26 November 1845, p. 1:5.

Reprinted: *New-York Weekly Tribune,* 29 November 1845, p. 1.

C 206
"The Ivory Christ." *New-York Daily Tribune,* 27 November 1845, p. 2:2.

Unsigned. Reprinted: *New-York Weekly Tribune,* 6 December 1845, p. 6.

C 207
"Ole Bull." *New-York Daily Tribune,* 28 November 1845, p. 1:1.

Reprinted: *New-York Weekly Tribune,* 6 December 1845, p. 6.

C 208
"Anniversary of the Polish Revolution." *New-York Daily Tribune,* 1 December 1845, p. 2:3–5.

Reprinted: *New-York Weekly Tribune,* 6 December 1845, p. 1.

C 209
Review of Frederick Von Raumer, *America and the American People. New-York Daily Tribune,* 4 December 1845, p. 1:1–3.

Reprinted: *New-York Weekly Tribune,* 13 December 1845, p. 6.

C 210
"Lyceum of New-Bedford, Mass." *New-York Daily Tribune,* 9 December 1845, p. 1:1.

Reprinted: *New-York Weekly Tribune,* 13 December 1845, p. 1.

C 211
Review of H. W. Longfellow, *Poems. New-York Daily Tribune,* 10 December 1845, p. 1:1–3.

Reprinted: *New-York Weekly Tribune,* 13 December 1845, p. 1; in "American Literature," *Papers on Literature and Art,* II, 150–159; *Art, Literature, and the Drama,* pp. 326–335; *The Writings of Margaret Fuller,* pp. 380–388; as "Longfellow's *Poems,*" *Margaret Fuller: Essays,* pp. 317–324.

C 212
"German Opera at Palmo's Opera House." *New-York Daily Tribune,* 11 December 1845, p. 1:1.

Reprinted: *New-York Weekly Tribune,* 20 December 1845, p. 6.

C 213
"Study of the German Language." *New-York Daily Tribune,* 11 December 1845, p. 1:2.

C 214
"Peale's Court of Death." *New-York Daily Tribune,* 13 December 1845, p. 2:2.

Reprinted: *New-York Weekly Tribune,* 20 December 1845, p. 1.

C 215
Anon. Fuller on Longfellow. *Broadway Journal,* 2 (13 December 1845), 359–360.

Reprinted from the 10 December *Tribune.*

C 216
"Books of Travel." *New-York Daily Tribune,* 18 December 1845, p. 1:1–3.

Review of Forsyth, *Italy;* Goethe, *Journey into Italy* and *Second Residence at Rome;* Pückler Muskau, *The German Prince;* and Waagen, *Works of Art and Artists in England.* Reprinted: *New-York Weekly Tribune,* 20 December 1845, p. 1; as "On Books of Travel," *Woman in the Nineteenth Century, and Kindred Papers,* pp. 286–287.

C 217
Review of T. Carlyle, *The Letters and Speeches of Oliver Cromwell. New-York Daily Tribune,* 19 December 1845, p. 1:1–4.

Reprinted: *New-York Weekly Tribune,* 27 December 1845, p. 6; as "Oliver Cromwell," *Life Without and Life Within,* pp. 179–190; as "Carlyle's *Cromwell,*" *The Writings of Margaret Fuller,* pp. 290–300.

C 218
"Lecture by Mr. Lane." *New-York Daily Tribune,* 19 December 1845, p. 2:2.

Reprinted: *New-York Weekly Tribune,* 27 December 1845, p. 6.

C 219
"Books for the Holidays." *New-York Daily Tribune,* 22 December 1845, p. 1:1.

Review of *The Complete Works of N. P. Willis* and Charles F. Hoffman, *The Vigil of Faith and Other Poems.* Reprinted: *New-York Weekly Tribune,* 27 December 1845, p. 1.

C 220
"Concert of Mr. Burke on Tuesday Evening." *New-York Daily Tribune,* 22 December 1845, p. 2:3.

C 221
Review of Mrs. H. F. Gould, *Gathered Leaves. New-York Daily Tribune,* 24 December 1845, p. 1:3.

Reprinted: *New-York Weekly Tribune,* 27 December 1845, p. 1.

C 222
Review of J. T. Headley, *The Alps and the Rhine. New-York Daily Tribune,* 24 December 1845, p. 1:3.

Reprinted: *New-York Weekly Tribune,* 27 December 1845, p. 1.

C 223
"Mr. Burke's Concert." *New-York Daily Tribune,* 25 December 1845, p. 1:3.

C 224
Review of William I. Kip, *The Christmas Holidays in Rome. New-York Daily Tribune,* 25 December 1845, p. 1:3.

Reprinted: *New-York Weekly Tribune,* 3 January 1846, p. 6.

C 225
Review of *Poetical Works of Percy Bysshe Shelley. New-York Daily Tribune,* 27 December 1845, p. 1:1–3.

Reprinted: *New-York Weekly Tribune,* 3 January 1846, p. 6; as "Shelley's Poems," *Life Without and Life Within,* pp. 149–152.

C 226
"1st January, 1846." *New-York Daily Tribune,* 1 January 1846, p. 1:1–3.

Reprinted: *New-York Weekly Tribune,* 3 January 1846, p. 1; as "First of January," *Life Without and Life Within,* pp. 207–218.

C 227
"Mr. Fontana's Concert." *New-York Daily Tribune,* 3 January 1846, p. 1:1.

Reprinted: *New-York Weekly Tribune,* 10 January 1846, p. 6.

C 228
Review of *Memorabilia of Swedenborg,* intro. George Bush. *New-York Daily Tribune,* 6 January 1846, p. 1:1.

Reprinted: *New-York Weekly Tribune,* 10 January 1846, p. 1.

C 229
"Mr. Fontana." *New-York Daily Tribune,* 6 January 1846, p. 2:3.

C 230
"Musselman Schools at Paris." *New-York Daily Tribune,* 8 January 1846, p. 1:1.

From the *Courrier des Etats-Unis.* Reprinted: *New-York Weekly Tribune,* 24 January 1846, p. 6.

C 231
"The Liberty Bell for 1846." *New-York Daily Tribune,* 9 January 1846, p. 1:1.

Reprinted: *New-York Weekly Tribune,* 17 January 1846, p. 6.

C 232
Review of Miss H. J. Woodman, *Sibylline Verses. New-York Daily Tribune,* 9 January 1846, p. 1:1.

Reprinted: *New-York Weekly Tribune,* 17 January 1846, p. 6.

C 233
Review of Schoolcraft Jones, *Ellen, or Forgive and Forget. New-York Daily Tribune,* 10 January 1846, p. 1:1–2.

Reprinted: *New-York Weekly Tribune,* 17 January 1846, p. 6; as " 'Ellen; or, Forgive and Forget,' " *Woman in the Nineteenth Century, and Kindred Papers,* pp. 269–275; as "A Further Caveat to Pastoralism," *Margaret Fuller: American Romantic,* pp. 219–221.

C 234
"Cassius M. Clay." *New-York Daily Tribune,* 14 January 1846, p. 1:1–2.

Reprinted: *New-York Weekly Tribune,* 17 January 1846, p. 1; *Life Without and Life Within,* pp. 326–329; *Margaret Fuller: Essays,* pp. 325–328.

C 235
"Der Volks-Tribun; Organ der Deutschen Sozial Reform-Association in New-York." *New-York Daily Tribune,* 17 January 1846, p. 1:1.

Reprinted: *New-York Weekly Tribune,* 24 January 1846, p. 1.

C 236
Review of Robert Wesselhoeft, *The Green Mountain Spring . . . Medical and Philosophical Communications. New-York Daily Tribune*, 17 January 1846, p. 1:1.

Reprinted: *New-York Weekly Tribune*, 24 January 1846, p. 1.

C 237
Review of John C. Warren, *Physical Education and the Preservation of Health* and Alexander Combe, *Treatise on the Physiological and Moral Management of Infancy. New-York Daily Tribune*, 19 January 1846, p. 1:1–2.

Reprinted: *New-York Weekly Tribune*, 24 January 1846, p. 1; as "Physical Education," *Life Without and Life Within*, pp. 116–120.

C 238
"Philharmonic Concert." *New-York Daily Tribune*, 20 January 1846, p. 1:1.

Reprinted: *New-York Weekly Tribune*, 24 January 1846, p. 1.

C 239
"Methodism at the Fountain." *New-York Daily Tribune*, 21 January 1846, p. 1:1–3.

Review of Thomas Jackson, *The Life of Charles Wesley*. Reprinted: *New-York Weekly Tribune*, 24 January 1846, p. 1; *Papers on Literature and Art*, II, 166–175; *Art, Literature, and the Drama*, pp. 342–351.

C 240
"Music." *New-York Daily Tribune*, 31 January 1846, p. 1:1–3.

Reprinted: *New-York Weekly Tribune*, 7 February 1846, p. 6.

C 241
"Publishers and Authors." *New-York Daily Tribune*, 3 February 1846, p. 1:1–3.

Review of Harro Harring, *Dolores*. Reprinted: *New-York Weekly Tribune*, 7 February 1846, p. 1.

C 242
"The Rich Man—An Ideal Sketch." *New-York Daily Tribune*, 6 February 1846, p. 1:1–3.

Reprinted: *New-York Weekly Tribune*, 14 February 1846, p. 6; *Life Without and Life Within*, pp. 287–296; *Margaret Fuller: Essays*, pp. 329–337.

C 243
"Leopold de Meyer." *New-York Daily Tribune*, 7 February 1846, p. 2:2.

Reprinted: *New-York Weekly Tribune*, 14 February 1846, p. 3.

C 244
Review of Pliny Earle, *Twenty-Fifth Annual Report of the Bloomingdale Asylum for the Insane. New-York Daily Tribune*, 11 February 1846, p. 1:1–3.

Reprinted: *New-York Weekly Tribune*, 14 February 1846, p. 1; as "Woman's Influence Over the Insane," *Woman in the Nineteenth Century, and Kindred Papers*, pp. 295–297.

C 245
Review of *Chronicle of the Cid*, trans. Robert Southey. *New-York Daily Tribune*, 12 February 1846, p. 1:1.

Reprinted: *New-York Weekly Tribune*, 14 February 1846, p. 1.

C 246
Review of T. Parker, *The Idea of a Christian Church*. *New-York Daily Tribune*, 13 February 1846, p. 1:1.

Reprinted: *New-York Weekly Tribune*, 21 February 1846, p. 6.

C 247
Review of L. Hunt, *Italian Poets*. *New-York Daily Tribune*, 18 February 1846, p. 1:1–2.

Reprinted: *New-York Weekly Tribune*, 21 February 1846, p. 1.

C 248
"The Rich Man—An Ideal Sketch." *Communitist*, 2 (19 February 1846), 105–106.

Reprinted from the 6 February *Tribune*.

C 249
"Prison Discipline." *New-York Daily Tribune*, 25 February 1846, p. 1:1–2.

Review of *Annual Report of the Inspectors of the Mount Pleasant State Prison, Second Report of the Prison Association of New-York, Third Annual Report of the Managers of the State Lunatic Asylum,* and *Report of the Pennsylvania Hospital for the Insane.* Reprinted: *New-York Weekly Tribune*, 28 February 1846, p. 1.

C 250
Review of R. W. Griswold, *D'Israeli's Curiosities of Literature, with Curiosities of American Literature*. *New-York Daily Tribune*, 25 February 1846, p. 1:3.

Reprinted: *New-York Weekly Tribune*, 7 March 1846, p. 6.

C 251
Review of Moritz Ertheiler, *Lecture on the Study of the German Language*. *New-York Daily Tribune*, 2 March 1846, p. 1:1.

Reprinted: *New-York Weekly Tribune*, 7 March 1846, p. 1.

C 252
Review of J. P. F. Richter, *Walt und Vult*. *New-York Daily Tribune*, 3 March 1846, p. 1:1.

Includes the reprinting of Fuller's poems on Richter in the July 1840 *Dial*. Reprinted: *New-York Weekly Tribune*, 7 March 1846, p. 1.

C 253
"Darkness Visible." *New-York Daily Tribune*, 4 March 1846, p. 1:1–3.

Review of George B. Cheever, *A Defence of Capital Punishment*. Reprinted: *New-York Weekly Tribune*, 7 March 1846, p. 1; as "Capital Punishment," *Life Without and Life Within*, pp. 199–206; *Margaret Fuller: Essays*, pp. 338–348.

C 254

" 'Darkness Visible'." *New-York Daily Tribune*, 10 March 1846, p. 1:1.

Reprinted: *New-York Weekly Tribune*, 14 March 1846, p. 1.

C 255

"Philharmonic Concert." *New-York Daily Tribune*, 10 March 1846, p. 2:3.

Reprinted: *New-York Weekly Tribune*, 14 March 1846, p. 1.

C 256

"Consecration of Grace Church." *New-York Daily Tribune*, 11 March 1846, p. 1:1–2.

Reprinted: *New-York Weekly Tribune*, 14 March 1846, p. 1; *Life Without and Life Within*, pp. 337–343; *Margaret Fuller: Essays*, pp. 349–351.

C 257

Review of *Twenty-Seventh Annual Report and Documents of the New-York Institution for the Instruction of the Deaf and Dumb. New-York Daily Tribune*, 18 March 1846, p. 1:1–2.

Reprinted: *New-York Weekly Tribune*, 21 March 1846, p. 1; as "The Deaf and Dumb," *Woman in the Nineteenth Century, and Kindred Papers* (1860 and subsequent printings), pp. 298–300.

C 258

"The Poor Man—An Ideal Sketch." *New-York Daily Tribune*, 25 March 1846, p. 1:1–3.

Reprinted: *New-York Weekly Tribune*, 25 March 1846, p. 1; *Life Without and Life Within*, pp. 297–303; *Margaret Fuller: Essays*, pp. 352–361.

C 259

"Instruction in the French Language." *New-York Daily Tribune*, 30 March 1846, p. 2:3.

C 260

"What fits a Man to be a Voter? Is it to be White Within, or White Without?" *New-York Daily Tribune*, 31 March 1846, p. 1:1–2.

Reprinted: *New-York Weekly Tribune*, 11 April 1846, p. 3; as "What Fits a Man to be a Voter? A Fable," *Life Without and Life Within*, pp. 314–318; *Margaret Fuller: Essays*, pp. 362–365.

C 261

"Browning's Poems." *New-York Daily Tribune*, 1 April 1846, p. 1:1–5.

Reprinted: *New-York Weekly Tribune*, 4 April 1846, p. 1; *Papers on Literature and Art*, II, 31–42; *Art, Literature, and the Drama*, pp. 207–218; *Woman in the Nineteenth Century, and Kindred Papers*, pp. 298–299.

C 262

"Discoveries." *New-York Daily Tribune*, 1 April 1846, p. 1:5.

Reprinted: *New-York Weekly Tribune*, 11 April 1846, p. 6; *Life Without and Life Within*, pp. 319–321.

C 263

"Remarkable Phenomenon." *New-York Daily Tribune*, 1 April 1846, p. 1:6.

Reprinted: *New-York Weekly Tribune*, 11 April 1846, p. 6.

C 264
"Wiley & Putnam's Library." *New-York Daily Tribune*, 4 April 1846, p. 1:1.

Review of H. Melville, *Typee;* William Makepeace Thackeray, *Notes of a Journey from Cornhill to Cairo;* La Motte-Fouqué, *Theodolf;* and *Aslauga's Knight.* Reprinted: *New-York Weekly Tribune*, 11 April 1846, p. 1; as "Typee," *Margaret Fuller: American Romantic*, pp. 221–223; as "Melville's *Typee*," *Margaret Fuller: Essays*, p. 366.

C 265
Review of *Payne's Universum, or Pictorial World. New-York Daily Tribune*, 7 April 1846, p. 1:1.

C 266
Review of *Le Franco-Americain. New-York Daily Tribune*, 7 April 1846, p. 1:1.

C 267
"Caroline." *New-York Daily Tribune*, 9 April 1846, p. 1:1–2.

Reprinted: *New-York Weekly Tribune*, 11 April 1846, p. 1; *Woman in the Nineteenth Century, and Kindred Papers*, pp. 250–255.

C 268
" 'Age could not wither her . . . '." *New-York Daily Tribune*, 10 April 1846, p. 1:2.

Reprinted: *New-York Weekly Tribune*, 18 April 1846, p. 1; as "Ever-Growing Lives," *Woman in the Nineteenth Century, and Kindred Papers*, pp. 256–260.

C 269
" 'Mistress of herself, though china fall'." *New-York Daily Tribune*, 15 April 1846, p. 4:1–2.

Reprinted: *New-York Weekly Tribune*, 18 April 1846, p. 1; as "Household Nobleness," *Woman in the Nineteenth Century, and Kindred Papers*, pp. 261–265; *Margaret Fuller: Essays*, pp. 367–370.

C 270
Review of *Scenes and Thoughts in Europe. New-York Daily Tribune*, 17 April 1846, p. 1:1–2.

Reprinted: *New-York Weekly Tribune*, 2 May 1846, p. 6.

C 271
"Condition of the Blind in this Country and Abroad." *New-York Daily Tribune*, 18 April 1846, p. 1:1–2.

Review of William Chapin, *Report on the Benevolent Institutions of Great Britain and Paris,* and *Sixth Annual Report of the Managers of the New-York Institution for the Blind.* Reprinted: *New-York Weekly Tribune*, 2 May 1846, p. 6.

C 272
Review of A. Dumas, *Comte de Monte Cristo. New-York Daily Tribune*, 18 April 1846, p. 1:2.

Reprinted: *New-York Weekly Tribune*, 2 May 1846, p. 6.

C 273
"Magnolia Conspicua." *New-York Daily Tribune*, 18 April 1846, p. 2:4.

C 274
"Wonders have not Ceased in our Times." *New-York Daily Tribune,* 24 April 1846, p. 1:1.

Reprinted: *New-York Weekly Tribune,* 2 May 1846, p. 6.

C 275
"Association. The Phalanstery about to be Introduced into Brazil." *New-York Daily Tribune,* 25 April 1846, p. 1:4.

Reprinted: *New-York Weekly Tribune,* 2 May 1846, p. 1.

C 276
"Romance and Reality." *New-York Daily Tribune,* 25 April 1846, supplement, p. 1:5.

From the *Deutsche Schnellpost.*

C 277
Review of Thomas Hood, *Poems. New-York Daily Tribune,* 25 April 1846, supplement, p. 1:6.

Reprinted: *New-York Weekly Tribune,* 2 May 1846, p. 1.

C 278
"Philharmonic Concert." *New-York Daily Tribune,* 28 April 1846, p. 2:3.

Reprinted: *New-York Weekly Tribune,* 2 May 1846, p. 1.

C 279
"Signor de Noronha's Concert." *New-York Daily Tribune,* 29 April 1846, p. 2:3.

C 280
Review Joel T. Headley, *Napoleon and his Marshals. New-York Weekly Tribune,* 2 May 1846, p. 1:3.

Reprinted: *New-York Daily Tribune,* 4 May 1846, p. 1.

C 281
"Mr. Walker's Concert." *New-York Daily Tribune,* 4 May 1846, p. 2:4.

C 282
"Francisco de Noronha to the Public and to his Friends." *New-York Daily Tribune,* 9 May 1846, p. 1:2–3.

Translated.

C 283
"Signora Pico's Concert." *New-York Daily Tribune,* 14 May 1846, p. 2:2.

C 284
"Christian Dancing, Christian Hunting, Christian Angling." *New-York Daily Tribune,* 16 May 1846, p. 1:1.

Includes a review of *The American Angler's Guide.* Reprinted: *New-York Weekly Tribune,* 30 May 1846, p. 6.

C 285
"A few Words in Reply to Mr. U. C. Hill." *New-York Daily Tribune*, 16 May 1846, supplement, p. 1:1–2.

C 286
"The Desert—By Felicion David." *New-York Daily Tribune*, 20 May 1846, p. 2:3.

Reprinted: *New-York Weekly Tribune*, 30 May 1846, p. 6.

C 287
"The Grand Concert." *New-York Daily Tribune*, 20 May 1846, p. 2:3.

C 288
"Victory." *New-York Daily Tribune*, 21 May 1846, p. 2:3.

Reprinted: *New-York Weekly Tribune*, 30 May 1846, p. 3.

C 289
"The Grand Festival Concert at Castle Garden." *New-York Daily Tribune*, 22 May 1846, p. 2:2.

Reprinted: *New-York Weekly Tribune*, 30 May 1846, p. 6.

C 290
"Le Franco-Americain." *New-York Daily Tribune*, 23 May 1846, p. 2:3.

C 291
"Methods of a Religious Life." *New-York Weekly Tribune*, 23 May 1846, p. 6:3–5.

C 292
Review of W. G. Simms, *Grouped Thoughts and Scattered Fancies* and *Areytos: or Songs of the South*. *New-York Daily Tribune*, 30 May 1846, supplement, p. 1:2–3.

Reprinted: *New-York Weekly Tribune*, 6 June 1846, p. 6.

C 293
Review of Hermann E. Ludewig, *The Literature of American Local History*. *New-York Daily Tribune*, 30 May 1846, supplement, p. 1:3.

C 294
Review of Theodore Leger, *Animal Magnetism: or Psychodunamy*. *New-York Daily Tribune*, 30 May 1846, supplement, p. 1:3.

C 295
Review of Eliza W. Farnham, *Life in Prairie Land*. *New-York Daily Tribune*, 30 May 1846, supplement, p. 1:4.

Reprinted: *New-York Weekly Tribune*, 6 June 1846, p. 3.

C 296
Review of Gabriel Surrenne, *The Standard Pronouncing Dictionary of the French and English Languages*. *New-York Daily Tribune*, 30 May 1846, supplement, p. 1:4.

C 297
Review of Waddy Thompson, *Recollections of Mexico*. *New-York Daily Tribune*, 2 June 1846, p. 1:1–2.

Reprinted: *New-York Weekly Tribune*, 6 June 1846, p. 1.

C 298

Review of J. Anthony King, *Twenty-Four Years in the Argentine Republic. New-York Daily Tribune,* 5 June 1846, p. 1:1–4.

Reprinted: *New-York Weekly Tribune,* 13 June 1846, p. 6.

C 299

Review of Henry T. Tuckerman, *Thoughts on the Poets;* Thomas Talfourd and James Stephen, *The Modern British Essayists;* George Gilfillan, *Sketches of Modern Literature and Eminent Literary Men;* and *A New Spirit of the Age,* ed. Richard H. Horne. *New-York Daily Tribune,* 10 June 1846, supplement, p. 1:2–4.

Reprinted: as "Critics and Essayists," *New-York Weekly Tribune,* 13 June 1846, p. 1.

C 300

"Belshazzar's Feast: An Attempt to Fulfill the Unfinished Design of Washington Allston by Thomas Spear." *New-York Daily Tribune,* 12 June 1846, p. 1:1–2.

Reprinted: *New-York Weekly Tribune,* 20 June 1846, p. 6.

C 301

Review of J. T. Headley, *Napoleon and his Marshals. New-York Daily Tribune,* 18 June 1846, p. 1:1–2.

Reprinted: *New-York Weekly Tribune,* 27 June 1846, p. 6; as "Napoleon and His Marshals," *Life Without and Life Within,* pp. 110–115.

C 302

Review of N. Hawthorne, *Mosses from an Old Manse. New-York Daily Tribune,* 22 June 1846, p. 1:1.

Reprinted: *New-York Weekly Tribune,* 27 June 1846, p. 1; in "American Literature," *Papers on Literature and Art,* II, 143–146; *Art, Literature, and the Drama,* pp. 319–322; *The Writings of Margaret Fuller,* pp. 375–377; as "Hawthorne's *Mosses from an Old Manse," Margaret Fuller: Essays,* pp. 371–374.

C 303

Review of G. Sand, *Consuelo. New-York Daily Tribune,* 24 June 1846, p. 1:1–2.

Reprinted: *New-York Weekly Tribune,* 27 June 1846, p. 1; as "From a Criticism on 'Consuelo'," *Woman in the Nineteenth Century, and Kindred Papers,* pp. 237–240.

C 304

Review of Edward Hazen, *Grammatical Reader,* and *Illustrated Botany. New-York Daily Tribune,* 26 June 1846, p. 2:5.

Reprinted: *New-York Weekly Tribune,* 4 July 1846, p. 1.

C 305

Review of Anna B. Jameson, *The Heroines of Shakespeare. New-York Daily Tribune,* 30 June 1846, p. 1:1.

Reprinted: *New-York Weekly Tribune,* 4 July 1846, p. 1.

C 306

"Colonel McKenny's New Book upon the Indians." *New-York Daily Tribune,* 4 July 1846, p. 2:4.

C 307
"Floral Fete for the Children of the Farm Schools on the Fourth July." *New-York Daily Tribune,* 4 July 1846, p. 2:4.

C 308
Review of Thomas L. McKenny, *Memoirs, Official and Personal. New-York Daily Tribune,* 8 July 1846, p. 1:1–3.

Reprinted: *New-York Weekly Tribune,* 11 July 1846, p. 1; as "Pochahontas," *Woman in the Nineteenth Century, and Kindred Papers* (1869 and subsequent printings), pp. 298–310.

C 309
Review of William Smith, *Memoir of Johann Gottlieb Fichte. New-York Daily Tribune,* 9 July 1846, p. 2:2.

Reprinted: *New-York Weekly Tribune,* 18 July 1846, p. 6.

C 310
"Browning's Poems." *New-York Daily Tribune,* 10 July 1846, p. 1:1.

Review of *Bells and Pomegranates VIII.* Reprinted: *New-York Weekly Tribune,* 18 July 1846, p. 6; *Papers on Literature and Art,* II, 43–45; *Art, Literature, and the Drama,* pp. 219–221.

C 311
Review of C. B. Brown, *Ormond* and *Wieland. New-York Daily Tribune,* 21 July 1846, p. 1:1–2.

Reprinted: *New-York Weekly Tribune,* 25 July 1846, p. 1; in "American Literature," *Papers on Literature and Art,* II, 146–150; *Art, Literature, and the Drama,* pp. 322–326; as "Brown's Novels," *Life Without and Life Within,* pp. 83–86; in "American Literature," *The Writings of Margaret Fuller,* pp. 377–380; as "Charles Brockden Brown," *Margaret Fuller: American Romantic,* pp. 223–227; as "Brown's Novels," *Margaret Fuller: Essays,* pp. 375–378.

C 312
Review of A. Dumas, *Count of Monte-Christo. New-York Daily Tribune,* 21 July 1846, p. 1:2.

Reprinted: *New-York Weekly Tribune,* 25 July 1846, p. 1.

C 313
Review of Anna B. Jameson, *Memoirs and Essays, Illustrative of Art, Science, and Social Morals. New-York Daily Tribune,* 24 July 1846, p. 1:1–2.

Reprinted: *New-York Weekly Tribune,* 1 August 1846, p. 6; as "Review of 'Memoirs and Essays, by Mrs. Jameson'," *Woman in the Nineteenth Century, and Kindred Papers,* pp. 288–294.

C 314
Review of C. Dickens, *Pictures from Italy. New-York Daily Tribune,* 24 July 1846, p. 1:2.

Reprinted: *New-York Weekly Tribune,* 1 August 1846, p. 6.

C 315
"School at Newton Centre, near Boston, Mass." *New-York Daily Tribune*, 31 July 1846, p. 2:1.

C 316
"Farewell." *New-York Daily Tribune*, 1 August 1846, p. 2:2.

Reprinted: *New-York Weekly Tribune*, 8 August 1846, p. 1; *Life Without and Life Within*, pp. 354–355; as "Farewell to New York," *Margaret Fuller: American Romantic*, pp. 250–252; *Margaret Fuller: Essays*, pp. 379–380.

C 317
Review of *Lyra Innocentium*. *New-York Weekly Tribune*, 1 August 1846, p. 1:1.

Reprinted: *New-York Daily Tribune*, 8 August 1846, p. 1.

C 318
Review of *Small Books on Great Subjects*. *New-York Weekly Tribune*, 1 August 1846, p. 1:1.

Reprinted: *New-York Daily Tribune*, 14 August 1846, p. 1.

C 319
"Study of the German Language." *New-York Weekly Tribune*, 1 August 1846, p. 1:2.

Reprinted: *New-York Daily Tribune*, 8 August 1846, p. 1.

C 320
"Green Mountain Spring." *New-York Weekly Tribune*, 1 August 1846, p. 1:2.

Reprinted: *New-York Daily Tribune*, 8 August 1846, p. 1.

C 321
Review of *The Treasury of History*. *New-York Weekly Tribune*, 8 August 1846, p. 1:2.

Reprinted: *New-York Daily Tribune*, 14 August 1846, p. 1.

C 322
Review of *Self-Formation*. *New-York Weekly Tribune*, 8 August 1846, p. 1:2.

Reprinted: *New-York Daily Tribune*, 12 August 1846, p. 1.

C 323
"American Literature," *New York Daily Tribune*, 23 September 1846, p. 1.

Reprinted from *Papers on Literature and Art*.

C 324
"Letters from England." *New-York Daily Tribune*, 24 September 1846, p. 2:1–3.

Letter of 23 August 1846. Reprinted: *New-York Weekly Tribune*, 26 September 1846, p. 1; *At Home and Abroad*, pp. 119–126.

C 325
"Things and Thoughts in Europe . . . II." *New-York Daily Tribune*, 29 September 1846, p. 1:1–3.

Letter of 27 August 1846. Reprinted: *New-York Weekly Tribune*, 30 October 1846, p. 1; *At Home and Abroad*, pp. 127–133.

C 326

"Things and Thoughts in Europe . . . III." *New-York Daily Tribune,* 24 October 1846, p. 1:2–3.

Letter of 20 September 1846. Reprinted: *New-York Weekly Tribune,* 31 October 1846, p. 1; *At Home and Abroad,* pp. 134–138.

C 327

"Things and Thoughts in Europe . . . IV." *New-York Daily Tribune,* 5 November 1846, p. 1:1–2.

Letter of 22 September 1846. Reprinted: *New-York Weekly Tribune,* 7 November 1846, p. 1; *At Home and Abroad,* pp. 139–146.

C 328

"Things and Thoughts in Europe . . . V." *New-York Daily Tribune,* 13 November 1846, p. 1:3–5.

Letter of 30 September 1846. Reprinted: *New-York Weekly Tribune,* 14 November 1846, p. 1; *At Home and Abroad,* pp. 147–157.

C 329

"De la Littérature Américaine," *La Revue Indépendante,* 6th yr., 2nd ser. (10 December 1846), 341–364.

French translation of "Elisabeth" Fuller's "American Literature" from *Papers on Literature and Art.*

C 330

"Things and Thoughts in Europe . . . VI." *New-York Daily Tribune,* 23 December 1846, p. 1:1–2.

Letter of November 1846. Reprinted: *New-York Weekly Tribune,* 2 January 1847, p. 1; *At Home and Abroad,* pp. 158–63; as "Poverty in England," *Margaret Fuller: American Romantic,* pp. 253–255.

C 331

"Things and Thoughts in Europe . . . VII." *New-York Daily Tribune,* 5 January 1847, p. 1:1–2.

Letter dated 1846. Reprinted: *New-York Weekly Tribune,* 9 January 1847, p. 1; *At Home and Abroad,* pp. 164–168.

C 332

"Things and Thoughts in Europe . . . VIII." *New-York Daily Tribune,* 2 February 1847, p. 1:1–3.

Letter of December 1846. Reprinted: *New-York Weekly Tribune,* 6 February 1847, p. 1; *At Home and Abroad,* pp. 169–175; as "Poverty in England," *Margaret Fuller: American Romantic,* pp. 255–256.

C 333

"Paragraph," *Literary World,* 1 (13 February 1847), 39.

Reprints part of Fuller's letter praising Joanna Baillie from the 2 February *Tribune.*

C 334
"Things and Thoughts in Europe . . . IX." *New-York Daily Tribune*, 19 February 1847, p. 1:1–3.

Undated letter. Reprinted: *New-York Weekly Tribune*, 20 February 1847, p. 1; *At Home and Abroad*, pp. 176–185; as "Carlyle," *Margaret Fuller: American Romantic*, pp. 257–259.

C 335
"Miscellany." *Literary World*, 1 (27 February 1847), 88.

Reprints part of Fuller's letter describing the Reform Club in London from the 19 February *Tribune*.

C 336
"Things and Thoughts in Europe . . . X." *New-York Daily Tribune*, 3 March 1847, p. 1:1–4.

Undated letter. Reprinted: *New-York Weekly Tribune*, 6 March 1847, p. 1; *At Home and Abroad*, pp. 186–196.

C 337
"Miscellany," *Literary World*, 1 (13 March 1847), 134.

Reprints part of Fuller's letter describing Carlyle from the 19 February *Tribune*.

C 338
"The Tragedy of Witchcraft." *Literary World*, 1 (27 March 1847), 183–184.

Reprinted without credit from *Papers on Literature and Art*.

C 339
"Things and Thoughts in Europe . . . XI." *New-York Daily Tribune*, 31 March 1847, p. 1:1–3.

Undated letter. Reprinted: *New-York Weekly Tribune*, 3 April 1847, p. 1; *At Home and Abroad*, pp. 197–203; *The Writings of Margaret Fuller*, pp. 409–410; as "Nature and Art," *Margaret Fuller: American Romantic*, pp. 265–268.

C 340
"Things and Thoughts in Europe . . . XII." *New-York Weekly Tribune*, 15 May 1847, p. 1:1–3.

Undated letter. Reprinted: *New-York Daily Tribune*, 19 May 1847, p. 1; *At Home and Abroad*, pp. 204–212; as "Rousseau," *Margaret Fuller: American Romantic*, pp. 268–269.

C 341
"Things and Thoughts in Europe . . . XIII." *New-York Daily Tribune*, 29 May 1847, p. 1:1–2.

Undated letter. Reprinted: *New-York Weekly Tribune*, 29 May 1847, p. 1; *At Home and Abroad*, pp. 213–219.

C 342
"Things and Thoughts in Europe . . . XIV." *New-York Weekly Tribune*, 31 July 1847, p. 1:1–3.

Letter of May 1847. Reprinted: *New-York Daily Tribune*, 5 August 1847, p. 1; *At Home and Abroad*, pp. 220–227; *The Writings of Margaret Fuller*, pp. 410–414.

C 343

"Things and Thoughts in Europe . . . XV." *New-York Daily Tribune*, 11 September 1847, p. 1:1–3.

Letter of 9 August 1847. Reprinted: *New-York Weekly Tribune*, 11 September 1847, p. 1; *At Home and Abroad*, pp. 228–235.

C 344

Linton, W. J. "Italy." *People's and Howitt's Journal*, 4 (9 October 1847), 527–528.

First printing of "To a Daughter of Italy."

C 345

"Things and Thoughts in Europe . . . XVII." *New-York Daily Tribune*, 27 November 1847, p. 1:1–3.

Letter of 18 October 1847. Reprinted *New-York Weekly Tribune*, 4 December 1847, p. 1; *At Home and Abroad*, pp. 242–249; *The Writings of Margaret Fuller*, pp. 416–422.

C 346

"Things and Thoughts in Europe . . . XVI." *New-York Daily Tribune*, 25 December 1847, p. 3:1–2.

Letter of October 1847. A footnote states that this letter reached the *Tribune* after no. XVII was published but should be designated as no. XVI. Reprinted: *New-York Weekly Tribune*, 25 December 1847, p. 1; *At Home and Abroad*, pp. 236–241; *The Writings of Margaret Fuller*, pp. 414–416.

C 347

"Things and Thoughts in Europe . . . XVIII." *New-York Daily Tribune*, 1 January 1848, p. 1:1–3.

Undated letter. Reprinted: *New-York Weekly Tribune*, 1 January 1848, p. 1; *At Home and Abroad*, pp. 250–256; *The Writings of Margaret Fuller*, pp. 422–428; as "Americans in Europe," *Margaret Fuller: American Romantic*, pp. 269–277.

C 348

"Things and Thoughts in Europe . . . XIX." *New-York Daily Tribune*, 29 January 1848, p. 1:1–4.

Letter of 17 December 1847. Reprinted: *New-York Weekly Tribune*, 5 February 1848, p. 6; *At Home and Abroad*, pp. 257–268; *The Writings of Margaret Fuller*, pp. 428–437.

C 349

"Things and Thoughts in Europe . . . XX." *New-York Daily Tribune*, 7 February 1848, p. 1:1–3.

Letter of 30 December 1847. Reprinted: *New-York Weekly Tribune*, 12 February 1848, p. 1; *At Home and Abroad*, pp. 269–275.

C 350

"Things and Thoughts in Europe . . . XXI." *New-York Daily Tribune*, 19 February 1848, p. 1:1–5.

Letter of 1–10 January 1848. Reprinted: *New-York Weekly Tribune,* 26 February 1848, p. 1; *At Home and Abroad,* pp. 276–291; *The Writings of Margaret Fuller,* pp. 437–448.

C 351
"Things and Thoughts in Europe . . . XXII." *New-York Daily Tribune,* 13 March 1848, p. 1:1–3.

Letter of 22–27 January 1848. Reprinted: *New-York Weekly Tribune,* 25 March 1848, p. 2; *At Home and Abroad,* pp. 292–302; *The Writings of Margaret Fuller,* pp. 448–451.

C 352
"Things and Thoughts in Europe . . . XXIII." *New-York Daily Tribune,* 4 May 1848, p. 1:1–3.

Letter of 29 March–1 April 1848. Reprinted: *New-York Weekly Tribune,* 6 May 1848, p. 1; *At Home and Abroad,* pp. 303–309; *The Writings of Margaret Fuller,* pp. 451–455; as "The Revolution," *Margaret Fuller: American Romantic,* pp. 278–279.

C 353
"Things and Thoughts in Europe . . . XXIV." *New-York Daily Tribune,* 15 June 1848, 1:1–5.

Letter of 19 April–13 May 1848. Reprinted: *New-York Weekly Tribune,* 21 June 1848, p. 6; *At Home and Abroad,* pp. 310–327; *The Writings of Margaret Fuller,* pp. 455–471; as "The Revolution," *Margaret Fuller: American Romantic,* pp. 279–280.

C 354
"Things and Thoughts in Europe . . . XXV." *New York Daily Tribune,* 19 January 1849, p. 1:1–3.

Letter of 2 December 1848. Reprinted: *New-York Weekly Tribune,* 27 January 1849, p. 1; *At Home and Abroad,* pp. 328–335; *The Writings of Margaret Fuller,* pp. 471–477.

C 355
"Things and Thoughts in Europe . . . XXVI." *New-York Daily Tribune,* 26 January 1849, p. 1:1–4.

Letter of 2 December 1848. Reprinted: *New-York Weekly Tribune,* 10 February 1849, p. 1; *At Home and Abroad,* pp. 336–345; *The Writings of Margaret Fuller,* pp. 478–486.

C 356
"What is Talked About." *Literary World,* 4 (27 January 1849), 84.

Reprints part of Fuller's letter stating her intention to write a book on the history of Italy from the 19 January *Tribune.*

C 357
"What is Talked About." *Literary World,* 4 (3 February 1849), 107.

Reprints part of Fuller's letter about the qualifications needed by the new U.S. ambassador to Italy from the 26 January *Tribune.*

C 358
"Varieties." *Literary World,* 4 (3 February 1849), 110.

Reprints part of Fuller's letter from the 26 January *Tribune.*

C 359

"Things and Thoughts in Europe . . . XXVII." *New-York Daily Tribune,* 31 March 1849, p. 1:2–4.

Letter of 20 February 1849. Reprinted: *New-York Weekly Tribune,* 7 April 1849, p. 1; *At Home and Abroad,* pp. 346–354; *The Writings of Margaret Fuller,* pp. 486–491.

C 360

"Things and Thoughts in Europe . . . XXVIII." *New-York Daily Tribune,* 4 April 1849, p. 1:1–3.

Letter of 20–24 February 1849. Reprinted: *New-York Weekly Tribune,* 14 April 1849, p. 6; *At Home and Abroad,* pp. 355–362; *The Writings of Margaret Fuller,* pp. 492–498.

C 361

"Things and Thoughts in Europe . . . XXIX." *New-York Daily Tribune,* 16 May 1849, p. 1:1–5.

Letter of 20–21 March 1849. Reprinted: *New-York Weekly Tribune,* 26 May 1849, p. 1; *At Home and Abroad,* pp. 363–379; *The Writings of Margaret Fuller,* pp. 498–503.

C 362

"American Artists in Italy, &c.," *Literary World,* 4 (26 May 1849), 458.

Reprinted from the 20 March *Tribune.*

C 363

"Things and Thoughts in Europe . . . XXX." *New-York Daily Tribune,* 23 June 1849, p. 1:2–4.

Letter of 27 May 1849. Reprinted: *New-York Weekly Tribune,* 30 June 1849, p. 1; *At Home and Abroad,* pp. 380–389; *The Writings of Margaret Fuller,* pp. 503–511; as "The Agony of the Revolution," *Margaret Fuller: American Romantic,* pp. 286–295.

C 364

"Things and Thoughts in Europe . . . XXXI." *New-York Daily Tribune,* 23 July 1849, p. 1:2–4.

Letter of 21 June 1849. Reprinted: *New-York Weekly Tribune,* 28 July 1849, p. 1; *At Home and Abroad,* pp. 401–409; *The Writings of Margaret Fuller,* pp. 512–521.

C 365

"Things and Thoughts in Europe . . . XXXII." *New-York Daily Tribune,* 24 July 1849, p. 1:2–4.

Letter of 10 June 1849. Reprinted: *New-York Weekly Tribune,* 28 July 1849, p. 1; *At Home and Abroad,* pp. 390–400; *The Writings of Margaret Fuller,* pp. 521–529.

C 366

"Chips from the Library." *Literary World,* 5 (28 July 1849), 69.

Reprints a selection from Fuller's writings under the title "Critical Praise."

C 367

"Scenes of the Siege—In Rome," *Literary World,* 5 (4 August 1849), 91–92.

Reprinted from the 10 June *Tribune.*

C 368

"Things and Thoughts in Europe . . . XXXIII." *New-York Daily Tribune*, 11 August 1849, p. 2:5–7.

Letter of 6–10 July 1849. Reprinted: *New-York Weekly Tribune*, 18 August 1849, p. 1; *At Home and Abroad*, pp. 410–421; *The Writings of Margaret Fuller*, pp. 529–539.

C 369

"Italy." *New-York Weekly Tribune*, 6 October 1849, p. 2:1–2.

Letter of 31 August 1849.

C 370

"Things and Thoughts in Europe . . . XXXV." *New-York Daily Tribune*, 9 January 1850, p. 1:2–3.

Letter of 15 November 1849. Reprinted: *New-York Weekly Tribune*, 12 January 1850, p. 1.

C 371

"European Affairs Discussed by Our Correspondents. Italy." *New-York Daily Tribune*, 13 February 1850, supplement, p. 1:2–3.

Letter of 6 January 1850.

C 372

"Recollections of the Vatican." *United States Magazine and Democratic Review*, 27 (July 1850), 64–71.

Signed "*" at the end of the article, "Countess Ossoli" in the table of contents.

CC. Supplement

Marginal Items

CC 1
"A Tale by Goethe." *Western Messenger,* 4 (December 1837), 217–234.

Unsigned. Translated. J. F. Clarke's headnote to the translation, while not mentioning Fuller by name, strongly implies her authorship.

CC 2
"To Allston's Picture, 'The Bride'." *Dial,* 1 (July 1840), 84.

"Signed "O." Reprinted (as part of the Allston Exhibition article): *Papers on Literature and Art,* II, 121; *Art, Literature, and the Drama,* p. 297.

CC 3
"A Sketch [I]." *Dial,* 1 (July 1840), 136.

CC 4
"A Sketch [II]." *Dial,* 1 (July 1840), 136.

CC 5
Untitled poem beginning, "Did you never admire . . : ." *Dial,* 1 (July 1840), 136.

CC 6
"Angelica Sleeps." *Dial,* 1 (October 1840), 172.

Translated.

CC 7
Review of Hermann Ulrici, *Ueber Shakspeare's dramatische Kunst und sein Verhältniss zu Calderon und Goethe. Dial,* 1 (October 1840), 272.

CC 8
Review of John Edward Taylor, *Michael Angelo, considered as a Philosophic Poet. Dial,* 1 (January 1841), 401–402.

CC 9
Review of Friedrich Krummacher, *The Little Dove. Dial,* 1 (January 1841), 405–406.

CC 10
Review of *Knight's Miscellanies. Dial,* 1 (January 1841), 406.

CC 11
Review of John Nichol, *Architecture of the Heavens, The Solar System,* and *The Structure of the Earth. Dial,* 1 (January 1841), 406.

CC 12
"Need of a Diver." *Dial,* 2 (July 1841), 53–55.

CC 13
Introductory note to "Cupid's Conflict." *Dial,* 2 (October 1841), 137.

CC 14
Review of William Motherwell, *Poems. Dial,* 2 (January 1842), 393–394.

CC 15
"Marie van Oosterwich." *Dial,* 2 (April 1842), 437–483.

Translated. Signed "A."

CC 16
Notice to correspondents. *Dial,* 2 (April 1842), 544.

CC 17
Review of *Life of Jean Paul Frederic Richter. Dial,* 3 (January 1843), 404–406.

CC 18
Notice of H. W. Longfellow, *Poems on Slavery. Dial,* 3 (January 1843), 415.

CC 19
Review of Fredrika Bremer, *The Neighbors. Dial,* 3 (April 1843), 532.

CC 20
"*Paracelsus.*" *Dial,* 3 (April 1843), 535.

Review of R. Browning, *Paracelsus.*

CC 21
Review of Heinrich Zschokke, *The Sleep Walker. Dial,* 3 (April 1843), 535.

CC 22
Anon. "A Peep Behind the Curtain." *Broadway Journal,* 1 (24 May 1845), 324–325.

Attributed to Fuller in James B. Reece, "A Margaret Fuller Satire on Longfellow," *Boston Public Library Quarterly,* 4 (October 1952), 224–227, but rejected for reasons listed in CC 25.

CC 23
"Wayside Notes Abroad . . . . No. I." *New-York Daily Tribune,* 8 August 1845, p. 1:2.

Signed "A.N." Fuller wrote James Nathan on 12 August that she had sent his travel letters to the *Tribune* for publication, and that they "did not need copying, and needed but little retouching, which I easily gave to your manuscript" (*Love-Letters,* pp. 141–142). She also commented that the printer had misread his initials. Reprinted (signed "J.N."): *New-York Weekly Tribune,* 16 August 1845, p. 1.

CC 24
"Wayside Notes Abroad . . . . No. II." *New-York Daily Tribune,* 8 August 1845, p. 1:2–3.

Signed 'A.N." Reprinted (signed "J.N."): *New-York Weekly Tribune,* 16 August 1845, p. 1.

CC 25
Anon. "The Whole Duty of Woman." *Broadway Journal,* 2 (23 August 1845), 101.

Attributed to Fuller, along with CC 22, by Reece, but both the style and the anonymous method of submission are totally unlike hers. John Ostrom, "Fourth Supplement to *The Letters of Poe,*" *American Literature,* 45 (January 1974), 526–527, says the letter accompanying this contribution and acknowledging authorship of CC 22, was "probably" by Fuller, although definitely not in her handwriting.

CC 26
"Wayside Notes Abroad . . . . No. 3." *New-York Daily Tribune,* 10 September 1845, p. 1:2.

Letter of 21 July 1845, signed "J.N." Reprinted: *New-York Weekly Tribune,* 13 September 1845, p. 1.

CC 27
"Wayside Notes Abroad . . . . No. 4." *New-York Daily Tribune,* 12 September 1845, p. 1:1–2.

Letter of 22 July 1845, signed "J.N." Reprinted: *New-York Weekly Tribune,* 20 September 1845, p. 1.

CC 28
"Wayside Notes Abroad . . . . No. V." *New-York Daily Tribune,* 16 September 1845, p. 1:1–2.

Letter of 23 July 1845, signed "J.N." Reprinted: *New-York Weekly Tribune,* 20 September 1845, p. 1.

CC 29
"Letter from Florence." *New-York Daily Tribune,* 2 December 1845, p. 1:1–2.

Letter of 25 September 1845, signed "J.N." Reprinted: *New-York Weekly Tribune,* 6 December 1845, p. 1.

Appendix / Index

Appendix

Principal Works About Fuller

Anthony, Katherine. *Margaret Fuller. A Psychological Biography.* New York: Harcourt, Brace and Howe, 1920.

Bell, Margaret. *Margaret Fuller.* New York: Charles Boni, 1930.

Braun, Frederick Augustus. *Margaret Fuller and Goethe.* New York: Henry Holt, 1910.

Brown, Arthur W. *Margaret Fuller.* New York: Twayne, 1964.

Buell, Lawrence. *Literary Transcendentalism: Style and Vision in the American Renaissance.* Ithaca: Cornell University Press, 1973.

Chipperfield, Faith. *In Quest of Love: The Life and Death of Margaret Fuller.* New York: Coward-McCann, 1957.

Deiss, Joseph Jay. *The Roman Years of Margaret Fuller.* New York: Crowell, 1969.

Detti, Emma. *Margaret Fuller Ossoli e i suoi corrispondenti.* Florence: Félice Le Monnier, 1942.

Durning, Russell E. *Margaret Fuller, Citizen of the World. An Intermediary Between European and American Literatures.* Heidelberg: Carl Winter, 1969.

Fuller, Richard F. *Chaplain Fuller.* Boston: Walker, Wise, 1864.

———. *Recollections of Richard F. Fuller.* Boston: privately printed, 1936.

Higginson, Thomas Wentworth. *Margaret Fuller Ossoli.* Boston: Houghton, Mifflin, 1884.

Howe, Julia Ward. *Margaret Fuller (Marchesa Ossoli).* Boston: Roberts Brothers, 1883.

Knortz, Karl. *Margaret Fuller und Brook Farm.* New York: Druck von Hermann Bartsch, 1886.

Myerson, Joel. *Margaret Fuller: An Annotated Secondary Bibliography.* New York: Burt Franklin, 1977.

Stern, Madeleine B. *The Life of Margaret Fuller.* New York: E. P. Dutton, 1942.

Thomas, John Wesley, ed. *The Letters of James Freeman Clarke to Margaret Fuller.* Hamburg: Cram, de Gruyter, 1957.

Wade, Mason. *Margaret Fuller: Whetstone of Genius.* New York: Viking Press, 1940.

Wellisz, Leopold. *The Friendship of Margaret Fuller D'Ossoli and Adam Mickiewicz.* New York: Polish Book Importing Company, 1947.

Index